TUFF JUICE

My Journey from the Streets to the NBA

CARON BUTLER

WITH STEVE SPRINGER

FOREWORD BY KOBE BRYANT

Guilford, Connecticut

An imprint of Rowman & Littlefield

Distributed by NATIONAL BOOK NETWORK

British Library Cataloguing in Publication Information Available

Library of Congress Cataloging-in-Publication Data

Butler, Caron, 1980-
  Tuff juice : my journey from the streets to the NBA / Caron Butler, with Steve Springer; foreword by Kobe Bryant.
      pages cm
  "Distributed by NATIONAL BOOK NETWORK"—T.p. verso.
  Includes index.
  ISBN 978-1-4930-1142-1 (hardcopy)—ISBN 978-1-4930-2382-0 (ebook) 1. Butler, Caron, 1980- 2. Basketball players—United States—Biography. I. Title.
  GV884.B88A3 2015
  796.323092—dc23
  [B]
                              2015024558

♾™ The paper used in this publication meets the minimum requirements of American National Standard for Information Sciences—Permanence of Paper for Printed Library Materials, ANSI/NISO Z39.48-1992.

This book is dedicated to my family

Thank You

Contents

Contents

Foreword

By Kobe Bryant

When we got Caron Butler in a trade prior to the 2002–2003 season, Laker general manager Mitch Kupchak gave him my phone number and Caron called me right away.

"Great to have you," I told him. "Ready to go work?"

He was ready. From the moment he stepped on the court at our El Segundo training site, he was totally focused, his competitiveness and no-nonsense attitude evident in everything he was asked to do.

That's all I needed to see. That's all I ever need to see from a teammate to appreciate him.

Caron and I bonded on day one and that bond remains as strong today as it ever was even though he now wears a different uniform.

Once I heard about Caron's background, where he started from, the obstacles that had been in front of him, the danger all around him as he grew up, I marveled at how far he had come, how much he had accomplished.

If I were going into battle, if I were going into a game where everything was on the line, I would want him with me. He's not afraid of the big moment, not afraid of an altercation, and I have a tremendous amount of respect for him because of that.

He was only twenty-four when he joined us, but he had already been face to face with potential disaster and death more times than most of us will confront in a lifetime.

That alters one's perspective. A lot of players, when they deal with crisis situations on the court, believe they are experiencing the ultimate pressure imaginable. But when you go through real things in your life, when you are tested time and again with far more at stake than just a victory or a defeat, your view of what constitutes pressure changes. That's something I learned from Caron. He's dealt with real pressure. He's dealt with life-altering situations. So when he steps on the court, nothing fazes him. To tell a teammate that he's not working hard, to challenge people at practice is nothing to Caron. He's challenged people who were carrying weapons.

Even though we were on the same team for only one season, we became very close. We were usually together on the road, going out to dinner or just hanging out. He has a great sense of humor, can take it as well as give it. I could hang out with him all day, go out and have a beer, watch games, or just talk.

With Caron, it even went beyond that. I became close to his family and he became close to mine. He came to my daughters' birthday parties.

When the Lakers were in Milwaukee for a game, he invited everybody on the team to dinner at his mother's house in Racine, twenty miles away. I went along with some of the other guys and we had a great time. Big cookout, lots of food, good music, and a chance to just hang out away from the normal road routine. That night, I felt like I was part of his family.

It's very rare for me to open up to somebody like that, but I just had a connection with him. He's one of my favorite teammates.

When that happens, it makes the season better. It doesn't always happen. It's not something that I need to have happen, but there are certain players that I just automatically get along with. You gravitate to each other because you see eye to eye on things and you get along extremely well. And Caron was one of those players.

There aren't many of them like that. There's Caron, there's Pau, there's D. Fish, and Ronnie Turiaf. That's four guys in a twenty-year career.

I still clearly remember the summer day in 2005 when the Lakers traded Caron. The day before, we had been working out together at our practice facility. We intended to follow that routine all summer and had big plans for the following season.

I was notified when the media was notified.

I was pissed to say the least. Pissed.

When we play against each other, I give him a big hug before the tipoff and have done so ever since the trade.

Caron has figured his life out thanks to his own perseverance and some great people who have served as mentors for him along the way.

I think it's wonderful that he is sharing with the world his phenomenal journey and the life lessons he has learned along the way through this book. Hopefully kids will read it and see something in it for their own journey. No two journeys are the same, although the emotional challenges each person faces are very similar. But they can see how he handled his challenges and perhaps find courage and bravery in their own dark moments.

I'm so proud of Caron. It's been a long time since he was a teammate, but it doesn't matter what uniform he wears. I view him like a brother and always will.

ONE

MY D-DAY: A DARK JOURNEY ENDS, A BRIGHT FUTURE BECKONS

It was such a short walk, merely seconds long.

Yet for me, walking from my seat in The Theater at Madison Square Garden up a few steps and across the stage to the podium was the triumphant finish of the toughest journey of my young life, a journey many predicted would end in disaster, and perhaps even death.

The date was June 26, 2002. The occasion was the NBA Draft.

Because Cher had a concert in the Garden, the smaller theater venue was being used for the draft. It created a more intimate setting, allowing me and the other projected top picks to be surrounded by family and friends. I had about fifty people there myself, most of whom had driven from Racine, Wisconsin, my hometown.

Sitting with me at the draft table were my mother, Mattie Butler Claybrook, my grandmother, Margaret Butler Bolton, my then-fiancee, Andrea, my brother, Melvin, my agent, Raymond Brothers, and Jameel Ghuari, who ran the neighborhood rec center in Racine and got me started in organized basketball.

It was the first time my grandmother, born and raised in Columbus, Mississippi, had ever been to New York.

I had smiled when I heard her initial impression of The Big Apple.

"People don't never go to sleep here," she said. "Every time you look out the window, somebody moving somewhere. People got things to do all night long."

Once the draft began, that smile had disappeared from my face. I was nervous as I watched NBA commissioner David Stern return to the podium time and again to announce the selections.

According to everything I had been told, I could expect to go anywhere from 3rd to 12th.

While you'd like to think your spot would be determined by what you did on the court, I learned that my place in the draft could also be affected by people who had never set foot on a college court. There are stats to be analyzed, wins and losses to be considered, attitude and work ethic to be examined.

But there is also the whisper campaign. Right after I left UConn, the very night of my farewell news conference, I had selected Raymond to be my agent. Other agents had interviewed me and filled my head with praise about how great my life story was, but when I didn't pick them, some of them tried to use my story against me to boost up their own clients.

Those agents would tell me, "We respect how you made it through all the hardships you endured, selling drugs and the gang activity. And now, that's going to work in your favor because team officials are not going to worry about you getting millions of dollars and messing yourself up. No, they will figure you've been through all that already. They are going to worry more about the kid who has never had any real money and, when drafted, is going to get exposed to it for the first time."

But when they had other clients who were potential lottery picks, those agents planted some bad seeds about me. They tried to damage my reputation by putting the idea in the heads of team GMs that my past might haunt my future.

It didn't work because I had been totally honest with every team I talked to. I told the team officials, "The reason I won't do this or do that is because I've already done it all. I don't have entourages. It's just me and my family. You can hire a private investigator or do whatever research you want. It's already all out there. It is what it is. I may have skeletons, but they are not hidden in my closet."

Yao Ming (from China) went first to Houston.
At No. 2—Jay Williams (Duke University) went to Chicago.
At No. 3—Mike Dunleavy Jr. (Duke University) went to Golden State.
At No. 4—Drew Gooden (University of Kansas) went to Memphis.
At No. 5—Nikoloz Tskitishvili (the country of Georgia) went to Denver.

Next up was Cleveland.

Three teams had invited me to work out for them: Memphis, Chicago, and Cleveland. I had a great workout in Cleveland and thought that was the place where I would wind up.

Then, I heard there was going to be a draft day trade involving the Cavaliers and the Clippers that would have sent me to L.A., but the Clippers botched it.

At No. 6—Dajuan Wagner (University of Memphis) went to Cleveland.

"Damn," I said to Raymond, "what's going on?"

With the selections rolling by, no teams reaching out to me, and seemingly all eyes in the room looking my way, I was sweating. My shirt was soaked all the way up my back underneath my suit coat. I had never worn a suit before, and I no longer wanted to wear one at that point. I started to take the coat off, but Raymond shook his head and told me to leave it on.

His cell was ringing constantly.

Every time it did, I asked, "Is that a team?"

And every time, Raymond replied, "Not yet."

At No. 7—Nenê Hilário (Brazil) went to New York.

Raymond motioned for me to get up and then led me into a nearby restroom. Once in there, he grabbed my hand and said we needed to start praying. He asked God to bless me, bless my career, and he wished for health for me and my family.

As we walked back to the table, the crowd started chanting, "Caron! Caron! Caron!"

When I sat back down, I looked at a nearby TV and heard Charles Barkley say I was the best player left in the draft.

Everybody around me was asking what I thought. I didn't know what to think.

At No. 8—Chris Wilcox (University of Maryland) went to the Los Angeles Clippers.

Raymond's phone rang again. As he listened to the voice on the other end, a smile broke out on his face. He gave me a thumbs up and said, "We good."

At No. 9—Amar'e Stoudemire (Cypress Creek High School, Florida) went to Phoenix.

No one else at the table knew that someone from the Miami Heat had called Raymond. But then the tension around me broke and the uncomfortable wall of silence was shattered by thunderous cheers as the commissioner told the crowd and a worldwide TV audience, "With the 10th pick in the 2002 NBA Draft, the Miami Heat select Caron Butler from the University of Connecticut."

I broke down and started crying. My mom started shaking. My grandmother started tearing up. And Andrea was smiling from ear to ear.

When I put my arms around my sobbing mother, she looked up at the ceiling and said, "Thank you, God. Thank you, God."

As I headed up the steps into the spotlight to shake the commissioner's hand and face the nation as a professional basketball player for the first time, my first thought was, "I made it. Now, don't fall."

Then, I started replaying the journey that had brought me here.

I thought about how far our family had come from the cotton fields of Mississippi.

I thought about the decades my grandmother had put in working at a tractor manufacturing plant in Racine, Wisconsin, to support my mother and her other children.

I thought about my mother working one, two, three shifts a day, piling up so many hours her nickname became "Overtime," all to make sure my brother and I would have a better life.

I thought about the rough streets of the south side of Racine where I sold drugs, dodged bullets, and first learned to dribble a basketball.

I thought about Junebug, once the drug kingpin of Racine, all the millions spent on crack cocaine, and all the wasted lives left behind.

I thought about my Uncle Carlos, whose dreams of college and a basketball career, of perhaps hearing his own name called in the draft, were destroyed by a drug bust that sucked him in and landed him behind bars even though he was an innocent man.

I thought about James Barker Jr., Andre King, and Black Rob, all close friends of mine who were shot to death.

I thought about all the other casualties of the gang wars I was a part of in the 1990s.

I thought about my mom driving down to the 18th Street park night after night to pull me out of that druggie hangout.

I thought about being arrested and locked up in the Ethan Allen correctional facility when I was fifteen with my mother spending much of my first night there outside the gates in her station wagon.

I thought about the time I spent in solitary confinement in Ethan Allen, alone with my Bible and my faith.

I thought about those dark days when I could have never even imagined making this walk up to shake the hand of the commissioner of the NBA.

I thought about the birth of my daughter, Camary Harrington, my first child, while I was in Ethan Allen.

I thought about the head of the Ethan Allen parole board who set me free even though I had to break the rules to get to him.

I thought about Detective Rick Geller of the Racine Police Department, who gave me the second chance my Uncle Carlos never had.

I thought about Jameel, who convinced me to join his AAU team and gave me a vision of what my world could be like if only I would cut my ties to the street life.

I thought about Max Good, a coach who took a chance on a kid with a troubled past, admitted me to a prep school in Maine, and taught me so much about basketball, and about life.

I thought about UConn basketball coach Jim Calhoun, who also gave me a chance when he had his pick of the litter with so many other talented high school stars elbowing each other to get in better position to make the UConn recruiting class.

I thought about my little brother, Melvin Jr., and how proud I was of him and his resolve not to follow the rocky road I chose growing up.

And I thought about Andrea, who had given me love, stability, and the hope for a normal family life.

As I reached the commissioner, he said, "Congratulations. How do you feel?"

I said, "Fucking great."

His eyes opened wide, he paused, and then he started laughing.

I repeated it: "Fucking great."

I was later told that, back home in Racine, cars were driving up and down the street, horns honking as if the town had just won the NBA championship.

I have to give a lot of credit to Raymond. He kept pitching my story, working it.

I think some teams were scared off early by my history, but Pat Riley, genius that he is, believed in my ability, believed in me as a person. He wasn't at the draft, but I talked to him by phone backstage. He said he was sending a private jet to pick me up and he'd see me in Miami.

After finishing up several media interviews, addressing a Heat draft party back in Miami on a video feed, and shaking hands with so many people that I felt like I was running for office, I started back down onto the floor of the theater. As I did so, I spotted Andrea's mother, Shirley, in the audience. Because Andrea's family is from Jamaica, they didn't know much about the NBA. They certainly didn't know anything about the draft. So Andrea made it very clear to me that if I wanted her mother's approval of our plans to marry, Shirley had to be at the draft.

"I need to bring my mom," Andrea told me, "because she needs to see that this is real, that it is something that can secure our future. Otherwise she is not going to let me leave with you. In her mind, you are just some boy without a job."

She may have stressed the importance of this day to her mom, but Andrea later conceded to me that she herself wasn't convinced it would be meaningful.

"It was the unknown," Andrea later told me. "I didn't understand it. I knew there are plenty of talented players who don't even get drafted. I was listening to you say you were going to be in the Top 10. I didn't know what the hell the Top 10 meant. I had never even watched the draft before."

That day, Andrea became a believer. So did her mom, who told her daughter after sitting in the audience and seeing the cameras and the crowd and the excitement, "Oh, this *is* something serious."

My mom didn't need convincing. She had always believed this day would come.

As she watched me at the podium, she thought about one of the many times she ordered me out of the park in Racine and into her car. On that particular occasion, I looked at her and said, "Mom, I am not going to get in trouble anymore."

While I didn't keep that promise right away, she clung to those words, sure I would eventually make good on that vow. And I did.

When I returned to the draft table, my mother told me with tears in her eyes, "This is so wonderful. It's one of the happiest days of my life. We don't have to live like we used to live anymore. I don't have to get up in the morning and work into the night. My head can stop being heavy. I ached so much it was like my body had a headache. That is going to disappear forever."

I went over to my grandmother, gave her a big hug, and told her, "We on our way now, Granny. We on our way."

TWO

MY ROOTS: THE COTTON FIELDS OF MISSISSIPPI

My family's roots run deep into the soil of Columbus, Mississippi, at the juncture of three rivers: the Tombigbee, the Buttahatchee, and the Luxapalila.

For more than two hundred years, settlers have been migrating there, taking advantage of federal land grants in the early days and building the farms and plantations that bordered the fertile Black Prairie soil, ideal for growing cotton.

After the Civil War, the lives of emancipated slaves often centered in a part of town known as Catfish Alley. It was there that many in the black community sold their produce and the catfish they had caught and hauled into town.

The sights and sounds of that community are the first my grandmother remembers. She was born in Columbus and lived in the city for the first five years of her life.

Then her mother, Mattie Lucille Butler, my great-grandmother, married Richard Butler, whose father, Sandy, owned eighty-two acres outside of town in a countryside crisscrossed by red-dirt roads. It was there that my grandmother spent her formative years.

When my family became members of the Butler clan, we joined a group that could have been a city in and of itself. In all, Sandy Butler had twenty-three kids. My grandmother always tells me, "We got people all over the world. Wherever you go, remember, someone is family."

My grandmother, her mother, and her three siblings, older brothers Roosevelt, Leroy, and Alonzo, moved into a big, white mansion. My grandmother can still remember walking in the front door and wandering down a huge hallway, her eyes bulging in awe as she looked up at the large paintings covering the walls on both sides.

As she soon learned, however, there wouldn't be much time for art appreciation. It was a working farm, complete with horses, pigs, and chickens, and everybody, including my grandmother, was expected to be part of the labor force. There was cotton, corn, okra, black-eyed peas, watermelons, and fruit off muscadine trees to harvest.

The descendants of slaves who had worked those fields and so many others throughout Mississippi and the rest of the South, denied freedom, wages, and basic human rights, had become the owners of many of those farms.

While her brothers and the other farmhands left a lot of their sweat in the field, my grandmother thought the work was fun.

At least at first.

Not so much fun was dealing with the snakes. They were everywhere on the farm, big, small, and often deadly. There were rattlesnakes, water moccasins, copperheads, eastern coral, redbelly, and mud snakes, to mention just a few.

"You name 'em, we had 'em," my grandma used to tell me.

She loves to repeat the story about the day her mother sat on a snake in their house, thinking it was just a cushion on the couch. My great-grandmother quickly realized something was wrong because cushions don't slither.

When she screamed and got up, the snake disappeared under the couch. It was lured out with sulfur, which snakes hate, and then killed with a shotgun.

The incident left a huge impression on my grandmother and a determination to avoid snakes whenever possible. As a young girl, she once ran three miles after seeing one.

The threat was a lot more serious after she became a mother. My grandmother married Johnny James Butler, a contractor who specialized in building homes. He was twenty-three; she was thirteen.

They soon had a family, an ever-growing family. In all, my grandmother had seven kids, five girls, including my mother, and two boys.

But motherhood didn't free my grandmother from working in the cotton fields. And with everybody working, there was no one to watch her babies. So my grandmother placed her infants on a quilt by the gate that led to the field. And while she picked cotton, she would constantly poke her head up to make sure no snakes had slithered onto the quilt to attack the helpless babies.

My mother remembers the house she lived in with her parents and siblings. The centerpiece was a potbelly stove, complete with legs, a feed door to insert wood or coal, and a flue pipe that ran up through the roof. "It was just like the stoves you see in Western movies," my mother would tell me.

She can still recall walking down a road while holding the hand of her brother, Richard, who was two years older. Behind them was my grandmother. All of a sudden, a snake came out of a ditch and got between my grandmother and her kids.

"Walk faster, Richard," said my grandmother, trying to stay calm.

And off Richard went, sister in hand, leaving the snake to wiggle off back into the ditch.

Just another day growing up in Mississippi.

A more terrifying memory from my mother's childhood comes from the day a huge flood hit the area, leaving her and her siblings stuck in a house that seemed on the brink of floating away.

All of a sudden, there was her father, my grandfather, arriving in a boat, picking up each of his children and getting all of them out of harm's way.

My grandmother's memory of him is not so warm and tender. Being his wife became an increasingly unpleasant experience as the years went by because my grandfather was a control freak.

"He was a very powerful man, used to doing what he wanted to do because he had money," my grandmother told me. "Instead of treating me like a wife, he treated me like I was a kid. There was no talking back. He was very demanding. I took it when I was thirteen years old, fourteen, fifteen, sixteen. On and on and on it went."

"Where you going today, Marvin?" my grandfather asked her one time. He always called her Marvin rather than Margaret.

"Well, I might go by the house of Miss Amy [his mother]," my grandmother said, "Or, I may stop by my mom's to pick up some collard greens and do the wash."

"I don't want you going nowhere today," he told her.

"Well, I'm going anyway," she insisted.

When my grandfather got home and found out she had indeed gone to her mother's house, he pushed my grandmother up against a wall and said, "Woman, when I tell you not to go nowhere, I mean for you to stay home till I get home."

The next day, she took off again.

And his response was the same, except it became more physical.

"You go down there to your mom's again," my grandfather said, "I'm going to show you what I'm going to do."

And he did show her, slapping her across the face.

My grandmother ran crying to her mother. "I am tired of Mr. Butler," my grandmother said. "I don't want to be married no more. I don't want to do what Mr. Butler tells me to do. I want to live my own life."

"I told you from the first not to marry him," her mother said. "He's older than you. He's more experienced than you. He's not going to treat you like an equal.

"Besides, Margaret, every other year, you are having a baby. You are not going to get away when you keep having babies. He is not going to let you leave."

While the beatings became more frequent, my grandmother became older and bolder. No longer an intimidated thirteen-year-old but a maturing woman heading into her twenties, she was finally able to confront my grandfather and tell him she was moving on.

"No you are not," he said.

"Yes I am."

"It's going to be just like a duck when you leave," my grandfather told her.

"Like a duck?"

"Whatever quacks, I'm going to shoot."

That threat melted my grandmother's resolve.

It would take some sort of life-changing event for her to finally split and, unfortunately, such an event did occur.

My grandmother's fifth child was a girl she named Darlene.

The baby came along at a time when my grandfather was beating my grandmother often and severely. Even when she was pregnant with Darlene.

Probably as a result, Darlene jerked her body violently at every sound as a newborn.

One day, Darlene grabbed my grandmother's wrist with as much force as her little hands could muster, became as rigid as a tree branch, and died in my grandmother's arms.

She was just three weeks old.

My grandmother had accepted her husband's blows for years, but the abuse that had resulted in the death of one of her children, even if it was an unintentional byproduct of her husband's wrath, was unacceptable.

She began talking about getting a gun.

She went to her mother and said, "Ma, I'm thinking about hurting him."

That did it.

Her mother told her, "Now you *are* leaving. We can't have you hurting somebody. We don't want you to end up in prison."

Where could my grandmother go?

The logical answer was Racine, Wisconsin, because there was already family there.

One of my uncles, Eugene Thornton, was the first in the family to leave Columbus, departing hastily one day in the early '60s.

He had no choice. I'm not sure exactly what he had done wrong, but I know the law was after him. According to family lore, his crime was sleeping with too many white women back then in mid-twentieth-century Mississippi.

Uncle Eugene didn't have a car and certainly didn't have the money to buy a plane ticket. That left him only one escape option: a bus. Law enforcement officers, of course, knew this, and so they staked out the bus stations.

They were looking for a young black man. They didn't pay attention to the young black woman who boarded a bus heading north. Only it wasn't a woman. It was Uncle Eugene wearing a wig and a dress.

If they had caught him, they might have killed him. But fortunately, Uncle Eugene got out of town, out of the state, and figured he'd keep heading north until he found a job. He could have stopped in Tennessee or Indiana or Illinois, but he kept hearing there were better paying jobs farther north. That led him to Wisconsin and to Racine, where the jobs were plentiful and lucrative. He went to work at the J. I. Case Co., manufacturers of farm machinery and other equipment. He left behind a girl named Mary who eventually joined him in Racine and became my Aunt Mary.

When word of the job opportunities reached Columbus, two of my grandmother's brothers, Leroy and Roosevelt, also headed north. In the fields of Mississippi, they had been making twenty-five cents a day. In Wisconsin, they worked in Racine at J. I. Case and in Kenosha at the Ocean Spray beverage plant. Leroy and Roosevelt had to lie to get hired since the minimum age for employment in both places was eighteen and they were sixteen and seventeen, respectively. They got away with it and started to make a decent living which, back then, was a couple of dollars a day.

Better than twenty-five cents.

When my grandmother was told she needed to get out of Columbus, she called Leroy in Racine and told him, "Bro, I think I'm going to hurt Jack."

Eugene, who had been in Wisconsin for a decade by then, told Leroy, "Go get her and bring her up here."

Easily said, but not so easily accomplished. Leroy couldn't afford to take more than a day off from J. I. Case. Racine and Columbus are situated 732 miles apart, a twelve-hour drive one way.

One day after work, Leroy hopped in his car, raced down to Columbus, picked up his sister and her kids, and roared back to Racine. He made the round trip of 1,464 miles so rapidly that it cost him only a single day of work.

By the time my grandmother arrived in Racine, she was twenty-three and had four young children. A fifth, my Aunt Kathy, was on the way.

"I glad we moved up here," my mother, six years old at the time, told my grandmother, "because, if we'd stayed in Mississippi, we probably would have gotten eaten by snakes."

THREE

MY GRANDMA: BREAKING BARRIERS AND DODGING BULLETS

When my grandmother came to Racine, she must have felt as if she had landed on another planet.

She had never seen snow before, never felt the force of a blizzard, never heard of temperatures being measured by the wind chill. She had never been away from her mother before, never been out of Mississippi, never even been out of the Columbus area. My grandmother had never done anything but pick cotton and other crops. And like her brothers, she had never made more than a quarter a day.

But my grandmother wasn't one to feel sorry for herself, or spend a lot of time reflecting on her life. With four kids and another one in her belly, there was too much to do.

She and her brood moved in with Leroy, his girlfriend, and their five kids. He had a two-story, four-bedroom house. That sounds nice, but it was small, very small.

My grandmother, my mom, her two sisters, and her brother, Richard, had to share one room. There were two big beds for the women, and Richard slept on a rollaway cot.

Despite being in her sixth month, my grandmother, grateful to have a roof over herself and her kids, did more than her share of the duties. She cooked every day for all twelve people in the house and cleaned up after all the kids and the family dog.

He was a German shepherd named Lightning. The thing my mom always remembers when she thinks of those days was how mean that dog was.

"The dog protected all of them," my mom said of Leroy and his family, "but not us. He would look at us and growl. He didn't bite us, but he acted like he wanted to. We were only in that house for six or seven months, but I guess it was six or seven months too long for him."

My mom would come in the kitchen and pull off a few scraps of meat from the dinner my grandmother was cooking.

"We would give it to Lightning," my mom said, "so he would be nice to us. But he never was."

Lightning wasn't the only one who thought my family had overstayed their welcome. My grandmother felt the same way. She hadn't left Columbus seeking her independence from my grandfather only to give it up so quickly upon arriving in Racine by depending on her brother for survival.

My grandmother was ahead of her time, a strong woman willing to do a man's work in order to be free to choose her own course in life.

And once she set that course, there was no way to change her mind. That's one of the many things I love about her.

Sure enough, soon after she had her fifth baby, my Aunt Kathy, on Thanksgiving Day, 1973, my grandmother took her kids and moved out.

Struggle was nothing new for her. She had lived through the turbulent days of the civil rights movement in Mississippi in the 1950s and '60s, ugly days when strong resistance to the end of segregation and Jim Crow laws was met with anger and violence.

It was different in Wisconsin in the 1970s. My grandmother was just one of thousands of blacks lured north by a widely expanding job market.

This was a state that, almost a century earlier, had been a pioneer in terms of racial equity. Born a slave, Peter D. Thomas became one of the first blacks in the entire country to hold public office when he was elected coroner of Racine County in 1887.

That didn't mean there was no history of racial discrimination in Wisconsin.

In 1900, twenty-five hundred blacks lived in the entire state, primarily in Racine, Milwaukee, and Beloit, a town located right on the border with Illinois. As employment opportunities for blacks exploded following the Great Depression and wages rose, the African-American population in the state increased 600 percent in a twenty-year period, from just over twelve thousand in 1940 to 74,546 in 1960.

Still, segregation was common in the job market. In 1965, six hundred people, blacks and whites, marched through downtown Racine to protest the mistreatment of African Americans. In 1967, protests were highlighted by the Freedom March.

Particularly galling was the blatant racism in the housing market. A black family looking through the real estate section of local newspapers could only consider houses that were listed as "Color Invited." Legislation outlawing discrimination in housing wasn't passed until 1968, following more protests and riots.

While the *Brown v. Board of Education* decision by the US Supreme Court in 1954 required the desegregation of public schools across the nation, it took another quarter century for that to become a reality in Milwaukee. It wasn't until 1979, following years of demonstrations and boycotts, that the city's school board implemented a desegregation plan, and that was a five-year plan.

There were many local leaders who led the fight for racial equality in Racine, names I admired when I read about them in school.

One who particularly stands out was Lloyd Jackson. It seemed like he was always knocking down some racial barrier, always expanding the role of blacks in Racine society. He was the town's first black school principal, taking over at Lakeside School in 1966. He was the city's first black alderman, elected in 1968. And he was the first black chairman of the Racine County Democratic Party.

There were others as well. Robert Turner, who started his political career when he was elected to the Racine City Council in 1976, went on in 1990 to become the first black man from Racine to be elected to the Wisconsin State Assembly.

And there was Corinne Owens, a black educator in Racine who was honored over the years by various organizations as Teacher of the Year,

Citizen of the Year, Woman of the Year, and the 1979 winner of the Rosa Parks Award.

They were all role models for me, demonstrating that, as an African American, I could be anything I wanted to be.

But my greatest role models were my grandmother and mother.

After my grandmother took her kids and moved out on her own, she went to work at J. I. Case, a company her brothers regarded as a gold mine for working people. She started out at $9.80 an hour in 1973.

She took her place among the men in the foundry on the assembly line for tractors and other farm equipment, proving to be every bit as tough, hardworking, and productive as her male counterparts.

My grandmother even worked the hot box, an iron device that heated up tractor parts. She had to stick her hands in the box, grab the boiling material, and file it down quickly enough to toss it onto a moving conveyor belt without missing her turn in the line of workers. She also did tractor repairs, installing transmissions and building alternators.

The working conditions were unhealthy to the point of being life threatening. The tractor parts contained all sorts of chemicals, causing her to breathe in toxic material.

For protection, my grandmother had to wear a respirator and specially designed safety shoes with protectors on the top to keep her from breaking her toes if a part fell off the assembly line.

Yet there she stayed, even through three more pregnancies, lasting thirty years on that assembly line. When she finally retired in 2002, she had amassed enough time on duty to get five years of severance pay.

As tough as that job was, my grandmother, with so many kids to raise, also had a second job at Ocean Spray, where she worked on the forklift, stacking boxes.

To see her go through all that taught me the value of a dollar. She was penniless when she left her brother's house to get a place of her own, yet provided for her ever-growing family for decades.

My grandmother never thought about going back to Mississippi to live, not even when she was told to do so at the point of a gun.

One day, two years after she had arrived in Racine, my grandfather showed up looking for her. He wanted my grandmother to go back to Columbus with him.

When she refused, my grandfather pulled out a gun and shot a bullet through our front door. He could have hit somebody in our hallway, but fortunately, no one was standing there at the time.

My mom called the cops and they quickly found my grandfather, the gun still in his hand.

"Yeah, I did it," he told the police, "because she wouldn't come back."

They escorted him to the train station and put him on the first train back to Columbus.

Despite my grandfather's attempt to shoot her, my grandmother would still take their kids back to Columbus to see him in the summertime. My grandmother would occasionally get to visit her parents and other relatives nearby, but most of the summer was spent with my grandfather, who had moved back in with his parents.

It was just like old times. My grandfather didn't want my grandmother to leave the house.

My Uncle Richard once told me, "I kept a relationship with my father after we came up to Racine. It wasn't really a good relationship, but it was a relationship. We didn't see eye to eye on nothing, but I did talk to him. My mother told me that my daddy used to hit her. I took that to heart, so that put a dent in our relationship. I couldn't be around nobody who was hitting my mother.

"But he was still my father, so I loved him."

FOUR

MY MOM: THE WOMAN THEY CALLED OVERTIME

My mother met my father at a Racine recreational center when my mother was fourteen. They soon broke up, but he left her with a surprise that would forever change her life. My mother was pregnant. She didn't find out until their brief relationship was history.

"We were both young," my mother has told me. "I wasn't trying to get pregnant. He wasn't trying to get me pregnant. It just happened."

My mom knew something was happening to her body, but at first, she wasn't quite sure what it was. How could any fourteen-year-old who had never been pregnant know what was occurring?

My grandmother took my mother to a doctor who diagnosed her condition as a bladder infection and gave her pills to clear it up.

Glad they didn't stay with that doctor. If they had, I probably wouldn't be here writing this book.

Once my mother's condition became evident, my father was furious. He was sure that she knew she was pregnant, but didn't want to tell him.

But that anger quickly faded, replaced by a desire to do the responsible thing by marrying my mother.

While she appreciated the offer, she told him she was too young to get married. She would continue to live under her mother's roof and grow into her own motherhood.

But she has admitted to me that she was scared to have a baby. She had just started to experiment with sex like her friends, and all of sudden, there I was.

I was born in St Luke's Memorial Hospital in Racine on March 13, 1980.

When it came to taking care of a baby, my mom was a quick learner, but she was glad that my grandmother was there to teach her. When I would cry at night, my grandmother, who certainly knew all about taking care of babies, would give me my bottle while my mother watched. Soon, my mom was taking over.

My dad left Racine before I was born and joined the Marines. Years went by before he and my mom spoke again. He didn't even know if his child was a boy or a girl until he finally met me when I was five.

We've seen very little of each other over the years. He doesn't come up in conversations I have with my family.

How do you miss a relationship you never had?

The first thing I can remember is my grandmother's house and a TV in the living room on top of another TV. There was a floor model that didn't work supporting a box TV. There were vinyl mats on the floor all through the house and plastic coverings on the furniture. I can still picture my grandmother cleaning the house, the smell of bleach everywhere. I also remember her washing clothes on a scrub board.

Her house, at 1937 Center Street on the south side of Racine, wasn't that big. It might have been twelve hundred or thirteen hundred square feet with three bedrooms and a basement. All seven of my grandmother's offspring lived there, including my mom, soon joined by me, the first grandchild in the house. Even though I was the nephew to all my aunts and uncles, I grew up like a little brother. When others in the family also started having kids, there were a ton of people living in that house, making it just as crowded as it had been when my grandmother moved in with Uncle Leroy.

My Uncle Richard was in and out of prison, and always bouncing around with different women when he wasn't behind bars, but my grandmother's place was always home for him. As the first born, he hovered over the family, watching out for us.

The sleeping conditions were rough. My grandmother had her own bedroom. Everybody else just found a spot to lie down at night. There would be two or three people in bed with me. Others would lie down on the couch in the living room or on the pull-out bed or just set a sheet out on the floor. We slept everywhere but the kitchen, but we made it work.

I didn't have my own bed until I was eight years old.

The first school I attended was Saint Rose, where I went for pre-school, kindergarten, and first grade. I have pleasant memories of that brief period of my life and the friends I played with, some of whom I later ran with on the streets. A portion of those memories, however, are tinged with sadness because too many of those childhood playmates didn't make it into adulthood, killed in the Racine drug wars of the '90s.

What I remember most about Saint Rose was how much time my mom spent there as a volunteer. The teenager who was scared to have me soon became my big protector, even watching over me in school because she was afraid to let me out of her sight. Since she was too young to work full-time, she would hang around my school, serving lunch to me and my friends, helping out with all the activities in the classroom and on the playground, always popping in, always hands on, always right there with me.

All my friends came from similar backgrounds, but their mothers weren't around like mine was all through my school years.

There is one memory from those days I'd like to forget. I had long hair and my mother used to send me to school with a blowout perm, causing many people to think I was a girl. Looking back, that probably made me tougher.

My favorite part of going to Saint Rose, indeed the highlight of my childhood, was leading the whole school in the Pledge of Allegiance over the loudspeaker from the main office. I wasn't shy. I would tell my mom I wanted to volunteer to do it and she would take me to the office to perform.

For me, poverty was part of growing up as far back as I can remember. I accepted it because it was always there, all around me.

Noontime for me as a kid meant it was time to go to Saint Rose School to get a free lunch long after I had been a student there. I would swing on the monkey bars in the playground while waiting for the long,

long line of unemployed or homeless folks to thin out so I could get my food. The local recreational centers also offered free lunches.

Thanks to my grandmother and then my mother, each of whom worked up to three jobs a day to keep us afloat, our household was better than most in the neighborhood.

Something else also kept us going: my grandmother's amazing luck. She was very successful gambling at the track on the horses and the grey-hounds. The majority of the time, she would win. That's how she bought the Cadillac that gave us vital transportation.

When other families didn't have dinner to put on the table, they would come to our house where my grandmother, already feeding her seven kids and me, would share with our hungry neighbors.

There were times when I didn't have anything to eat, but my aunts and uncles would always give me a piece of their portion. When one of us broke bread, we all broke bread. That was something that I learned at an early age, something that my grandmother taught in her house.

It's a philosophy I follow to this day. When I have successful moments in my life, when I sign a new contract or win a big game or get a pres-tigious honor, I try to incorporate my whole family into the celebration because that's how I was brought up.

I spent a lot of time with my grandmother, and she taught me so much about all sorts of things, especially life. She talked to me about mat-ters that most adults wouldn't mention to kids. She'd say, "This bill is due and we can't afford to pay it," or "Uncle Richard went to jail. He's facing this amount of time in prison because of drugs."

With so many of us living in such a small area, the conversations were for everybody. There wasn't any filter in the house. I was hearing honest communication among adults at seven, eight, nine years old. I grew up fast because I was exposed to those frank discussions. The attitude was, "We speaking on this shit and everybody is going to learn from it. If you learning from it now, good. If not, you'll go through it yourself."

I also learned, from early childhood on, that a lot of things I wanted, we simply couldn't afford. I understood my mother's body language when she was trying to tell me, you can't have this or you can't have that. I knew how much it hurt her to deny me. I saw her frustration.

I was frustrated as well. I felt deprived. It made me bitter when I saw kids on television, especially on commercials, living a life my friends in the neighborhood couldn't even imagine. Those kids wore new clothes, without a tear in them, rode fancy bikes, and played with shiny new toys. I'd see kids on scooters, or sending remote-controlled airplanes into the sky, or flying a kite.

A kite.

Nobody ran around flying kites in my neighborhood. I wondered where in the hell they got all that stuff? It seemed like those things didn't really exist.

I'd watch kids playing on a beach on TV. I'd never even seen a beach in person.

At least, it was just on TV. That made it easier to accept. It wasn't like kids were running by my house with all those toys, throwing them in my face while all I could do was press my nose against my front window and watch.

The only time I saw people with nice things in our community, I knew they had those possessions only because they sold drugs or were involved in other illegal activities to get the upper hand.

I saw crimes committed all the time as a kid while riding down the street on my Big Wheel. I shouldn't really call it riding because the Big Wheel was no longer big by then, or even much of a wheel anymore. It had been worn down to its core, so I would have to stand on my front leg and push my pathetic little three-wheeler with my back foot to get around the neighborhood. What I saw were drugs being sold and kids dodging cars driven by the young drug dealers, most of whom didn't even have a driver's license and were constantly getting into accidents, often leaving their wrecked cars embedded in trees, walls, or light posts.

I definitely felt white people lived on an entirely different planet than we did as a black community, a whole other world. It was a world I thought I couldn't connect with, certainly didn't belong to, and never would. I always felt different.

At that point in my life, none of my impressions of white society, based solely on what I had been taught about it, were good.

All I ever heard as a child was, "We weren't treated right in Mississippi because of white folks. We worked in a cotton field because of them and all they would ever give us was a quarter a day. We finally got run out of Mississippi because of white folks. We suffered from racism."

I was never told that we owned many of the cotton fields ourselves and were free to make our own fortune.

I was told that, once we came up to Wisconsin, a predominately white state, my uncles went to jail.

"The white lawyer didn't do your Uncle Richard right. He also wasn't treated right because it was a white judge and he was hard on your uncle because he was black." That's what I heard, not that Uncle Richard got caught selling drugs and was on the wrong side of the law.

There were never any good conversations in my house about white people. They were pretty much bashed on a daily basis by the adults around me.

Now some of it was certainly justified. I would hear that we had to march for this or that because white people were denying blacks some basic rights in our society and nobody can argue that wasn't true.

Again, TV showed me the difference between the two societies. It was white people I saw driving the new cars, owning the car dealerships and other businesses, and having perfect families like the one I saw on *The Brady Bunch*.

I also watched *Mork and Mindy*, *The Honeymooners*, and *I Love Lucy*. All I saw were white people in all the major roles. White people everywhere. I didn't see any program starring anyone of color until *227* and *The Jeffersons* came into my living room.

The only place I felt equal was in my dreams. There, I could live the childhood I desperately wanted. There, I was free. I dreamed big, dreams where I'd be able to have everything I wanted. We'd be in a big house and my grandmother and my mother didn't have to work. The sun was shining. We were enjoying life, going places together. I'd dream of Mississippi, seeing all my family reunited, smiling and enjoying each other's company.

I'd dream of riding on bicycles with all my cousins, laughing, having those kinds of moments I'd see on TV.

Then I'd wake up and I'd still be on Center Street. It was back to my world and what I had to deal with. I'd get up and go to Saint Rose or the rec center to get a free lunch. Reality sunk back in rather quickly.

At least when it came to clothes, I was covered adequately. My grandmother would take us to the open, flatbed Goodwill truck because she had a relationship with someone who worked for Goodwill. Or sometimes, we would jump on the Salvation Army truck. They had a massive load of items piled up. We would wade through the stuff and find fabrics. Once in a while, we would go to Value Village, a third-hand clothing store. Not second hand, but third hand. You could buy jackets and socks there, and all sorts of other items to wear. That's how I got my clothes. It wasn't the best stuff, but it did the job.

Anything was better than seeing my mom arrested for shoplifting as she once was, a really bad moment that I'll never forget.

I understand why it happened. She would do whatever was required to make sure I didn't have to go without clothes on my back, even if it meant breaking the law. To her, it was about survival.

I didn't realize what my mom was doing at first. During a period when all of our options for clothes had temporarily shut down, she took me to the mall and into a dressing room at one of the department stores. She told me to wait there and then came back with four pairs of pants and five shirts. She said to put them on, all of them at the same time.

When I looked at her with a quizzical expression, as if to say, "What are you doing?" my mom replied calmly, but firmly, "Just put these on." Then, I'd walk out of the store. That was back-to-school shopping for me.

One time, she and I wound up running through the mall after a security guard realized what was happening. My mom hoped I would have blacked out that incident in my memory by now, but I remember it clearly.

One of the security guys yelled out, "Ma'am, stop!" My mom pushed me aside and ran in the opposite direction, hoping they wouldn't associate me with her.

Somehow, I made it out of the mall, worn out and sweating from running with all those layers of clothes on me. I found our car and waited there, scared they had caught her and taken her away, leaving me alone with no way to get home.

They didn't catch my mom that day. She showed up at the car, quieting my rapidly beating heart.

But another time, my mom did get caught. They arrested her and took me into protective custody. The family came to get me, but she went to jail. When she got out, she promised me she would never do that again.

She never broke that promise.

My mom didn't take me to the malls with her again to get me clothes or steal any items, but she always made sure I had what I needed because she had another promise to keep, the promise to always be there for me.

Though still a teenager, the experience in jail caused my mom to quickly mature. It helped to be living with the perfect role model in my grandmother, who had been working since she first stepped into a cotton field as a child.

So my mother dropped out of school, went to work, and didn't stop until I reached the NBA. When she was sixteen, she cleaned houses, two in one day. When she turned eighteen and was legally able to hold a job, she took me, four years old by then, moved out of my grandmother's house, rented a place for us, and began working for various companies in different positions. My mom had jobs at Wendy's, at Western Publishing, at Color Art, at the Chicken Factory, where she plucked chickens, and at InSinkErator, the world's largest manufacturer of residential kitchen garbage disposals.

Those are just the jobs that stand out in my memory, but she had a lot more. And it was always more than one at a time. She'd work a day job, then one in the early evening and, at times, a third job in the middle of the night. She would bounce around through temp services. She'd work at one place and, boom, leave for the next job. She was trying to make it happen.

And she did.

To me as a kid, my mom's most fascinating job was forklift driver. She had learned it from my grandmother, the two of them proving they could do anything a man could do. My mom ran the forklift in two warehouses. They contained all sorts of products packed into boxes that sat on pallets. Using the forklift, she would stack those pallets five high and then transfer them to semitrucks when it was time to ship them out.

My mom did all that without even owning a license to drive the forklift. It's not that she wasn't willing to apply for one, nor proven, I am sure, to be as qualified as any other driver in the company. But her boss told her that she didn't need the license. Maybe he was worried because she was a woman or because she was too young. But that didn't stop him from putting her on that forklift whenever there were trucks to be loaded.

That was only one of my mom's duties. She was also in charge of "palletizing" everything, as she called it. She would keep track of the number of boxes on each pallet, repack products from damaged boxes, wrap them all tightly, and make sure they were all shipped on time and to the proper destination. And she kept the warehouse clean and neat in her "spare" time.

She would work that job from 7:00 a.m. to 3:30 or 4:00 in the afternoon. Then she would go to A & E Incorporated, a tool company, where she assembled wrenches and other tools on an assembly line.

Finally, my mom would clean several apartments, working until midnight or 1:00 a.m. She would laugh when I asked why she had to work a third job, saying it was the easiest thing she did all day.

My mom eventually replaced the cleaning jobs by going to work at InSinkErator, where she was on another assembly line, this time putting together garbage disposals from 11:00 p.m. to 7:00 a.m.

Sometimes she worked seven days a week, eighty hours in all, never turning down an opportunity for overtime.

Most of the guys at InSinkErator didn't even know my mom's real name because everybody called her Overtime.

"I've never seen a woman work as much as you do," one coworker told her. "Every time I turn around, you are here. It's like you live here. You have done more overtime than anyone I ever knew."

Fortunately, she had a lot of energy and was in good shape. She stood 5'11" and weighed less than 130 pounds.

Still, my mom would admit to me that, at times, she was "rest broken."

For a while, she got a welfare check from the government and food stamps. But eventually, she lost those benefits because she was making too much money. That was acceptable to her. She would rather work any day than take a handout, even from the government.

At least my mom never had to worry about paying to leave me at a day-care center or with a babysitter. Between my grandmother and my aunts, she had round-the-clock babysitters. Whether it was picking me up from school or taking me to the doctor or the dentist, there was always somebody available since we all lived within a two-block radius of each other.

While it was great to spend so much time with my grandmother and all my aunts and uncles, yet still maintain our own family unit—me, my mother, and my little brother, Melvin Jr., when he came along—in a separate house, that put a further financial burden on my mom.

I remember coming home from school and seeing eviction notices in the form of a pink slip on the door. A few times, I got to them before my mother did.

I'd ask, "Mom, what's this?"

She'd say in a casual tone, "Oh no, the landlord messed up."

He must have messed up a lot because, month after month, those pink slips would be there.

When the landlord, Ed Kanick, would come over, we'd have to make it seem like no one was home. All three of us got down and got quiet. But it wasn't as simple as that because, while we had shades or blinds on all the windows, they were so thin that, if anybody stood up, their silhouettes could be seen moving around from the outside. So my mom put up sheets that covered all the windows. Those sheets were so effective that someone trying to peek in couldn't even see the shades and the blinds. We did that for years.

She would come up with just enough money to buy us some time. "I owe 400," my mom would tell the landlord. "Here's 250. I'll get the other

150 next month." We were always behind. Shit, I think we were behind until I went into the NBA.

My mom was supposed to mail the rent. I recall times when she would drive to the landlord's house and put a money order in his mailbox because her payment was so late. She would also include a note, apologizing that the full amount was not there and giving him a date when she could pay in full.

He was a great landlord, because he never kicked us out even though there were many times when he would have been justified in doing so. Instead, he would move us to another of the many properties he owned around town rather than putting us on the street. Over the years, we stayed in three of his houses, all in different neighborhoods.

He always took care of us.

Sadly, he was killed when he got run over in a car accident in downtown Racine.

One day, after my mom had worked a twelve-hour shift, she came home and collapsed into her beloved recliner chair. Nine years old at the time, I came over and started rubbing her aching legs.

"Momma, your legs hurt?" I asked.

"No," she insisted, "I'm just tired."

"One day," I told her with a big smile on my face, "I'm going to get a really, really good job, making a lot of money. I'll be like Michael Jordan. And then, I'm going to buy you a brick house and a brand-new car."

She smiled back, gave me a big hug and a kiss, and said, "Thank you, baby. I'm going to be so happy when that day comes."

FIVE

MY DRUG-DEALING DAYS: FROM CRUMBS TO KANGOLS

I first learned about drugs at the age of seven in Winslow Elementary School. We were taught the importance to our health and well-being of living in and helping to maintain a drug-free environment.

I knew drugs were harmful to people, something that could ruin their lives. I knew you could go to jail for possessing them. In addition to the teachers at Winslow, I learned how deadly drugs could be from my mom and from McGruff the Crime Dog.

A nationally known crime prevention mascot, McGruff starred in a series of TV commercials in which he always uttered his famous motto, "Take a bite out of crime." A performer portraying McGruff came to Winslow several times to warn us about the dangers of crime. Wearing a trench coat along with a dog's head, the performer looked more like Inspector Gadget to me. He was invited as part of a local program called Cops 'N Kids, geared toward warning us at an early age about the consequences of breaking the law. He talked to us about the importance of staying off the streets, and avoiding gangs and the temptation of drugs. If you see someone who could harm you, we were told, be aware.

I knew exactly who the McGruff character was talking about. Winslow was a drug-free zone, but once I got out in the neighborhood, I saw the crack dealers. Even as a young child, I knew what a drug dealer looked like. And I wanted nothing to do with those people. The message from my mom, my teachers, and McGruff was a powerful one and I got it. I made it very clear to everyone around me that I would never sell drugs.

And yet, as I got a little older, it became a mixed message in my mind. Yes, drug dealing was wrong, very wrong, but, on the other hand, the people who were successful and had money in my neighborhood were the people who sold drugs.

At that age, I thought the only place in Racine where you could get drugs was on State Street on the north side. I got that idea from going there one time with my mom when I was a youngster. It was a block filled with take-out chicken places and check-cashing businesses. My mom had driven over there because she had a check to cash.

While she took care of her transaction, I remained in the back seat of the car, looking around. As I did so, my eyes got as big as silver dollars as I saw all the activity around me. There were women on the street who were not fully dressed. I saw guys with beepers hanging off their waists and gold chains hanging around their necks. I saw cars with gold rims around their tires. There were no cell phones in those days, but I remember seeing guys at the various pay phones on the block.

And I saw people who were broken down, pathetic, seemingly withering away. Those were the dope fiends.

When my mom got back in the car and saw me peering out the window, she told me, "Stay away from here. Don't you ever come back to State Street."

I nodded in agreement. State Street was a bad place. But I figured there would be no reason to ever go back there, because State Street was a long way from my house. At least it seemed like a long way to a young kid, but remember, all of Racine is only seven miles long.

I was nine years old the first time I encountered someone actually using drugs.

I was in the living room of my house and my mother's boyfriend at the time was in the kitchen in the back. My mom, knowing what he was up to, ordered me to stay in the living room or go to my room. Wanting no part of his addiction, she then went into her bedroom and shut the door.

There was no way I was going to listen to her. You tell a kid, especially a nosy one like me, not to go into a room because there's something going on in there that he shouldn't see, guess what he's going to do? Head right to that room, of course.

I tiptoed up to the kitchen door and peeked around the corner. There I saw a needle sticking in the boyfriend's arm, and rather than looking like he was in pain, he was just nodding out.

When you're a kid, you never want to get a shot, never want a needle to go in you unless you get some Twizzlers licorice from the doctor afterward.

Even now, all these years later, I can still see that needle stuck in that arm because it was so shocking to me. Just like seeing someone get shot or experiencing a funeral for the first time, that visual will always be in my head. Coming around the corner and encountering that is something I will never forget. At the time, I thought I would never see that again.

I figured out what he was doing instantly, but I thought, "Damn, why is he shooting it in his arm? That's not how they do drugs. This must be a new way." I didn't get it. In movies, you see people snorting or tasting cocaine.

Now that I'm familiar with drugs, I realize the boyfriend was shooting up either coke or heroin.

Seeing him slouched over, I thought, "Wow, that must be some powerful stuff."

I vowed right then and there that I was never going to do that.

It was quiet for about twenty or thirty minutes in the house after I tiptoed away, maybe longer. I had gone back into the living room to watch Michael Jackson on TV.

When the boyfriend finally came out of the kitchen, there was purpose in his stride. Gone was the stupor that had enveloped him. He was a different person, but not a better one.

He confronted my mother and demanded to know where the money was that he claimed to have given her. When she said he hadn't given her anything, he started pulling out drawers, ripping sheets off the bed, demanding to know where she had put the rent money. He was desperate. He needed cash and he needed it now.

I couldn't understand what the hell was happening to him.

Looking back now, I realize he needed more drugs. He had the itch. That quickly, he had developed a craving for another hit. Wanted it so bad, it was making him crazy.

I thought, "Wow, that's what drugs do to you?"

My mother never did drugs. By being with this boyfriend, she was settling. She could have done a lot better, and eventually, she did when she married my stepfather, Melvin Claybrook.

It wasn't long before I experienced my first hands-on experience with drugs. My friends would get Bible paper—yes, they actually ripped pages out of a Bible—or real thin paper they could buy in a store, sprinkle tobacco or marijuana on the paper, and roll it up.

After we went to the neighborhood center and got our free lunch, we would often head to a nearby lake. One day, one of my friends handed me a piece of that rolled-up paper and said, "Smoke this. It's a reefer."

The older kids would be down there with handguns. They'd sit on the rocks and shoot into the water. Those were the cool things to do, smoke pot and shoot bullets into the lake.

That's what I did as a nine-year-old, along with my buddy, David McAllister, who lived next door. We'd shoot pistols with the older dudes.

That was some crazy shit we were doing. It was Bam! Bam! Bam! Then we'd go play basketball or bounce around on the swing set. That was the way we grew up.

As I got a little older, my friends and I started to admire the neighborhood superstars. In my neighborhood, the superstars were the drug dealers.

The most powerful of those superstars was Junebug. I knew him personally and boasted about that to my friends. His real name was Jimmy Carter; he was dating my Aunt Kathy and was involved in drug dealing with my Uncle Richard, but Junebug was the biggest drug dealer any of us had ever met, ever even seen. Uncle Richard made so much money selling drugs that his nickname on the streets was Daddy Rich, but it was Junebug who seemed larger than life. Everybody on the south side talked about him. He was making several hundred thousand *a week*, had three or four cars with rims on them, including gold rims on one car that cost $50,000, owned enough gold jewelry to open his own store, and had a crew of twenty to thirty people working for him, all driving Cadillacs. Junebug had the newest this, the newest that. It seemed like he had everything.

He once won a BMW in a dice game. He shut down the local Foot Locker one day and bought out most of the merchandise in the store. He used to throw money around, giving it away. He would go into a bar and buy everyone a drink. He called himself "The Santa Claus of the ghetto."

He certainly had the keys to the city.

Once asked if he put all his money in a bank, Junebug replied, "Man, in this town, I am the bank."

He would stash his money under floorboards or planks in the attic, in drainpipes, or in other hidden spots around his house, his mother's house, grandmother's house, a sister's house, and our house. Then, if he wanted to buy a car, he'd go around the neighborhood, picking up $10,000 in cash from one hiding place, $20,000 from another, and on he'd go until he had enough for the purchase price.

Be like Mike? Everybody I knew wanted to be like Junebug.

To us, he was even bigger than Michael Jordan or any of the other basketball stars we watched on TV, because Junebug was someone we could actually see in person, touch, and talk to. That was more satisfying than getting an autograph from somebody who barely acknowledged your existence.

Junebug was in his early twenties at the time. He seemed older because we were so young, but at the same time, he was someone we could relate to because he was younger than most of the parents we knew.

His nickname came from a childhood fascination with the many grasshoppers he found on the sidewalks near his house. His siblings gave him the name Junebug, but, as he got older, it no longer seemed amusing to him. He preferred J. B. Once he started selling drugs and bringing in the big bucks, the name turned into J. B. Money. That he liked.

Like me, Junebug grew up in Racine, and started selling drugs in his early teens. His heroes were older drug dealers like James "Superman" Barker and Harlem. Once Junebug started shooting dice or gambling with them, he saw they had unlimited funds and drove sharp cars like the Excalibur.

When he learned their money came from drug dealing, he saw a path that could lead to unimaginable riches for himself as well. It seemed a lot easier than getting a real job.

"Easy bucks," Junebug told himself.

His parents weren't there to stop him. His mother was always gone. His father? Turned out, as Junebug later discovered, that his pop was also selling drugs. That's how the old man was able to afford fancy wheels of his own.

Once he decided to get involved in the drug trade, Junebug, showing organizational skills at an early age, set up an operation with a formal structure. He enlisted the buddies that he grew up with in the neighborhood to form the core of his team. Then he recruited players from his basketball team, telling them, "Hey, forget basketball. It's cool, but I need you all to come with me and make some money, real good money." He wound up initially with fifteen guys under his command. People familiar to me like Steve, Chubby, Kurt, and Shorty all worked for Junebug.

He set up a drug house on a Racine street, a one-stop drug shopping center he called "The Spot." Once the south side addicts learned about The Spot, they lined up around the corner to get the merchandise.

The operation was well organized, efficient, and largely fail-safe. Junebug's crew members all had roles and specific work hours, coming in for either the early-morning, afternoon, or evening shifts.

When a customer approached the house, those inside were alerted by outside sentries equipped with walkie-talkies. When the customer, usually a male, knocked on the door, it was opened by a doorman who directed the person to a hallway. Only one customer at a time was permitted in that hallway, where he could shop for an item within his price range.

Another crew member would emerge from the shadows with samples of cocaine on a plate. The customer would make his selection and place his money on the plate. It was the gangster version of a jewelry store. The man with the plate would take out his share of the purchase price and then take the plate over to the doorman, who would approve the sale, conclude the transaction, and send the buyer on his way.

Next customer.

Policemen cruising by could certainly see the line stretching all the way down the block, but the only way they could raid The Spot was by obtaining a search warrant. And that would require having proof that drugs were being sold in there.

"I could have a thousand people in line," Junebug told me, "and only be serving dinners."

The only way the cops could get the coke they needed as evidence was to pay an informant to go in and buy it. The informant would take it to the police, who would take it to a judge who would give them the warrant.

That all took time. So if Junebug had a suspicious customer, an unfamiliar face acting nervous or poking his nose around the house as if he were memorizing the layout, Junebug was able to prepare for a visit by law enforcement officers.

By the time he got a walkie-talkie warning, telling him, "Police coming," he had a bucket of acid ready by his side. When the police came barreling in, the coke went into the bucket. All gone without a trace.

That worked as long as Junebug sold the cocaine in powder form that could be snorted to get a high. If the junkies wanted to turn it into the harder rock form, what we all call crack cocaine, in order to smoke it, they had to cook the coke.

Crack cocaine made Junebug and other big-time dealers nervous because it was harder to dissolve in case of a raid, and the penalty for selling it was much stiffer if they got caught.

But Junebug eventually had to alter his thinking because the suppliers started selling it to him in rock form, the younger dealers sold it that way, and the addicts soon demanded it. The marketplace had changed.

"You can sell it faster," the suppliers told him, "if I give it to you cooked up."

The whole process sped up. The addicts could buy the crack on the streets, go sit in their cars, stuff the coke into their pipes, smoke it until they had inhaled every last ember, then go back out on the street and buy some more.

The lines at The Spot soon disappeared. The action was on the street or at the 18th Street park, drug central on the south side.

It was a game changer. Junebug was going to have to adjust and he did, expanding his operation throughout the neighborhood.

But as his organization grew, his own involvement shrunk. More than ever, he played the role of kingpin, maintaining strict control while keeping his distance. "The quicker you get rid of the drugs," he told me, "the less chance there is of getting caught by the police. And if I'm not personally selling it, I can't get caught at all."

In the beginning, Junebug, like most drug dealers, figured he'd only be in the business short term anyway, make some money, satisfy his material desires, and get out before he wound up behind bars or in the morgue, the inevitable destinations for those who stay in for the long haul.

But as the money came pouring in week after week, month after month, he was, as he explained, "bit by the buzzard."

Determined as Junebug thought he was to get out, he found he couldn't walk away from all that money or the lifestyle.

He told me, "I always said, when I made $50,000 or $100,000, I was going to quit. I'm an inner-city kid, so, to me, $50,000 was a lot of money. But when you get it, and it comes so quick, it seems like nothing compared to what you could get. You might spend $50,000 on a car and some rims, and it's all tax free. So now, you want a hundred thousand. You want a million. Suddenly you got garbage bags full of money, fast money coming at you hand over fist. It was my way out of the ghetto. You are thinking, 'Man, this is the life.'

"How are you going to turn your back on that? If all you've ever done is sell drugs, what else can you do? But if you don't have the business knowledge about what to do with all that money—and how could you if you were never taught—it's going to destroy you."

Junebug did have business sense. When people came to him to borrow a few hundred dollars until payday, he would give it to them, but tack on some interest. Or if they were desperate, he would buy their food stamps, but only pay half of what they were worth.

It was Junebug who inspired me to become a drug dealer. When I saw him bringing garbage bags full of money into the basement of our duplex to be divided up among his crew, I decided that was the life for me as well.

It all started for me one night when I was eleven years old. I had to get up at 3:00 in the morning in those days because I had a newspaper route, delivering the *Racine Journal Times*. My stack of papers would be thrown onto my lawn around that time from a company truck. I would have to pull out the sports and entertainment sections and put them together with the front section to make up the full newspapers I would deliver. My mom had helped me do that until she started working through the night. Then, I was on my own.

I was alone when Junebug and some of his guys came into the house that night with their cash-laden garbage bags.

When I was younger, I'd see Junebug early in the night as he headed out the door onto the street. He'd tell me, "Keep an eye on your cousins," meaning his own kids, "and when I come back, I'll toss you some cash." He'd give me a wink and he'd be gone. By the time he returned, I'd be long gone into dreamland.

But now, a little older and responsible for the paper route, I was wide awake, watching every move by Junebug and his crew with fascination.

Several of his guys stayed outside in the front and back of the duplex. Pulling the shades aside enough to peek out, I could see they were carrying guns as they patrolled the premises. They were obviously protecting those who had gone down into our basement with Junebug to divvy up the drug money.

As I was wrapping rubber bands around my newspapers, the crew came up upstairs, laughing about the big haul they had collected on the streets.

One of them saw me crouched behind a pile of newspapers, in awe at the stacks of money the guys were carrying. He gave me a big smile and tossed me the bag of crumbs he was holding. "Crumbs" is the term used to describe the residue of cocaine, what's left after it's cut up. It may have been crumbs to Junebug's gang, but to me, it was a mother lode. It weighed about seventeen grams.

And so it began.

There was never any doubt what I was going to do with those crumbs. Not after seeing how much money Junebug and his guys had brought home that night.

I will never forget how excited I was as I divided that bag up into smaller bags. I decided I would sell each one for $20, earning me $600.

I owned a bike, but I used a little red wagon to deliver my papers, throwing them onto the lawns and porches of houses throughout the neighborhood. I carefully placed the bags of coke on the bottom of my wagon and then covered them up with the newspapers.

I decided to finish my paper route first, then get started on my exciting new business.

Usually, people hit the streets with three or four bags of coke, and if the police come, the dealers swallow the merchandise. But being a novice, I had thirty bags on me, so if the police had come, I would have gone straight to a juvenile detention center.

So there I was, the papers all delivered, just sitting on the street at the crack of dawn, trying to figure out how to proceed. I couldn't exactly set up a stand like I was going to sell lemonade.

There were people passing by, the strange types of people who walk around in the middle of the night in bad neighborhoods. Remember, I was only eleven and getting real nervous.

Finally, I thought, "Fuck this, I'm going back to the house."

As I started walking fast, pulling my wagon full of cocaine behind me, scared of every shadow and strange sound, this guy suddenly appeared, walking straight toward me. He was in his thirties, tall, slender, with a curl hairdo.

"You holding, little man?" he asked me. "You holding?"

"Yeah," I replied. "What you looking for?"

"What you got?"

I pointed to the thirty bags in my wagon and told the man it would cost him twenty bucks a bag.

He claimed he only had $40 on him. He threw the money on the sidewalk and grabbed four bags.

I was satisfied. I had just made my first drug sale.

I thought, "I just got $40. On this paper route, I get $100 for *three* weeks worth of work. And I just made $40 for walking up the damn street. Oh yeah, I could make a career out of this."

By the time I got home, my mom was there, but Junebug and the other guys were gone. I didn't dare tell her what I'd done.

I skipped school the next day, staying on the streets instead to sell the rest of my coke bags. Didn't tell her that, either.

I wound up making about $400. I spent half of it on some Nike shoes. I was a dope man wearing my dope man shoes. That's what they used to call them on the streets. I also bought a fresh pair of Levi's, a white T-shirt, a gold-plated gun belt, and a Kangol hat, the furry type worn by the old-school drug dealers.

I felt official, a real drug dealer. I was doing it. "You're making money now," I told myself. "It's on."

I wasn't worried that my mom would figure out what I was up to, because she knew that, at times, Junebug or Uncle Richard would throw me some money or buy me clothes. So it wasn't alarming to her to see me with all my new gear. One time when she did ask me where I was getting the money for my clothes, I told her I had made it by babysitting my cousins for my aunt and Junebug.

I was the youngest guy in the neighborhood dealing drugs, but the cops didn't suspect me because of my *Journal Times* job. They would say, "Oh, that kid. He works hard. He's a good boy. He stays off the streets. He's cool."

I was cool all right.

Junebug didn't know what I was doing. If he was the supermarket for drugs in Racine, I was just the corner store. I wasn't even worth his attention. When he and his crew counted their money from the garbage bags, it took hours. I could hold my cash in my fist. He was selling ounces up to kilos. I was selling crumbs.

Some guys sold bags for $20, $40, or $50 depending on the neighborhood and the clientele. The bigger dealers would sell one-sixteenth of an ounce, an eighth of an ounce (called an "eight ball"), a quarter-ounce, a half-ounce, an ounce, or a kilo. Those heavier quantities were called "weight." Much bigger stuff than what was found in my little bags.

A kilo was the largest amount sold, heavy, heavy stuff. It was referred to as "weight-weight." To me, it was Junebug weight. A kilo would go for $17,000, maybe $17,500, on the street.

It would be naïve to think that, with all the money drug czars like Junebug were making, nobody in Racine would decide that the easiest path to riches led to his doorstep.

Sure enough, at 7:30 one morning, as he and my Aunt Kathy, by then his wife, were coming downstairs from their place, the top level of the duplex we shared, two men, armed and masked, ran out from behind the building and grabbed them.

My aunt started screaming, but before anyone could hear her, the attackers, waving guns, ordered her and her husband to go back upstairs, where they were tied up, Junebug in the front room, my aunt in a bedroom.

"Where is the money at?" the intruders yelled at her.

They had already grabbed the $10,000 in cash that was scattered out in the open.

Junebug wasn't concerned about the money. He called that "chump change." What he and my aunt were worried about were their three kids, all of whom were still asleep in their rooms.

Junebug had fathered only one of the three, but considered all of them his children and they, in turn, all called him Dad.

The robbers had seen Junebug's convertible parked outside, complete with $50,000 gold rims and a $10,000 sound system.

"Where's the keys?" they asked.

"I don't have them," Junebug said. "They are downstairs."

"Who lives downstairs?" the home invaders wanted to know. "We want to go down there." They figured there must also be more money down there.

Downstairs was our place where my mom, my brother, and I lived.

The masked intruders pulled Junebug out of the chair in which he had been tied, dragged him outside, motioned toward our front door below, and told him to go down there and knock.

"If we go down there," said Junebug, thinking quickly, "the mother is going to cause a big scene. Believe me, she's going to go off when she sees you young punks with masks on. You are going to have to kill her."

That was a line one of the robbers did not want to cross. So, he grabbed Junebug by the collar and yanked him back into the upstairs apartment. He and his partner tried to get my aunt to go down, but she refused.

My mom had just gotten home from an all-night shift at one of her many jobs. If she had found those two intruders in our apartment threatening my brother and I, they would have had to shoot her to stop her from protecting us. Nobody was going to mess with her babies.

Those two guys wanted no part of her. They weren't so kind to Junebug. They went down to their car, pulled out a can of gasoline they had stored in the trunk, came back up, and poured it on him as he sat back in the chair, still tied up. As Junebug gasped for air, they threatened to drop a lit match on him unless he came up with car keys and some more money.

My mother had seen the robbers' van parked in the back as she got home from work, but didn't think that was unusual because she knew strangers were always going up those stairs to buy drugs from Junebug. But the smell of gasoline coming from above was unusual. Maybe somebody had spilled gas on the floor of her sister Kathy's place, but why would there even be gasoline in the apartment? My mom was trying to decide whether to call Kathy for an explanation, yell upstairs, or simply go up there. Fortunately, my mom didn't get a chance to act because her thoughts were interrupted by an ear-piercing scream.

It was coming from a terrified Kathy. Seeing her husband doused in gasoline with a match shoved in his face pushed her over the edge. Freaking out, she screamed so loud and long, they probably heard her down at the police station several blocks away.

"Enough is enough," she kept yelling.

The two robbers had had enough of Aunt Kathy. They took the $10,000 and took off, loose bills flying out of their hands as they stumbled down the stairs.

To this day, I laugh when my mother tells people, "If you smell gas, call 911 right away, even if it's coming from your sister's house."

There were other instances where people came after Junebug with guns in search of his fortune and his stockpile of drugs. There were a few shootouts, but they never got him.

Even in my own little universe, the more money I made, the more I started thinking somebody might try to take it away from me. I heard about people getting shot for their drug money. I decided I needed some protection. I needed a gun.

It wasn't hard to find one. People were selling guns all over the south side. One guy was selling them out of his house for $50 to $100 each.

I asked one of my cousins to go over there for me. Nobody would sell a weapon to an eleven-year-old.

"What the hell do you need a gun for?" my cousin asked me.

"Don't worry," I told him. "It's not for me. I'm asking for somebody else."

He looked at me suspiciously, so I told him to forget it. I was going to have to find a way to get one myself.

My chance came after I turned twelve when I bumped into a fourteen-year-old, drug-dealing dude.

"Heard you was looking for a gun," he said.

I nodded my head.

He sold me a snub nose .32 revolver along with four bullets for $100.

I got me a gun.

Junebug got his cache of drugs from suppliers who came out of Chicago and Milwaukee. You have to have a reputation for being reliable, consistent, and productive in the drug trade to get guys like that to work with you. You need them a lot more than they need you.

At first, I got my coke from Junebug's crew. The people who were selling the heavy weight for him sold me the smaller stuff. I met them at my house, at truck stops, wherever we could get some privacy.

Even though Junebug was part of the family after he married my Aunt Kathy, I still had to make my case to get in on the action. "I'm a good worker," I'd tell them. "I'm making money. I'm flipping the stuff fast."

I would pay them for half of what they gave me and they would usually front me the other half. Back then, if a supplier gave me a quarter-ounce of crack, it cost me $225 to $250, but I could make $600 to $700 depending on whether he gave me shredded crumbs or ready rock. If I got it in soft crumbs, I had to cook it to make it hard and sometimes, when I did that, I lost grams. If I got it already rock hard, I knew exactly what I was getting. I would break it down and divide it into bags. I wouldn't take what I got and sell it in one chunk, because my customers couldn't afford that much. They were small time compared to Junebug's clients.

But that meant a lot more risk to me. People who sell weight, meaning a whole ounce or a kilo, at one time are less exposed than a guy who sells bags. By selling weight, they are limiting the number of people who are going to see their face because only a handful of customers can afford the cost. Thus, they limit their chances of getting caught. The easiest transaction is selling a kilo for $17,500. But who the hell has $17,500?

When I sold bags, I was exposed to everybody. I was out there on the corner selling to this guy, and that guy, and another guy. There was no way of telling if any of those guys were informants.

While the suppliers were happy to front me the money for the second half of the purchase, they made it very clear, family or no family, that I had accrued a debt and it would be paid promptly. "So next time I see you," they would say, "you'd better have the money."

I wasn't concerned because the drugs went quickly. I never had trouble getting rid of the stuff. Never. I could sell an ounce in a couple of hours. I'd take a couple of ounces and sell them in the same day.

I'd carry a pager back then before cell phones, and as soon as the last ounce was gone, I'd be on that pager, telling my supplier, "Come back. I need more! I need more!"

They'd get back to me real quick.

There were times when I couldn't sell drugs, but that wasn't because I was having trouble finding takers. It was because the supply had temporarily run dry. We called that a drought.

I'd run into the neighborhood drug fiends wandering around aimlessly like dogs who had lost their masters. "Damn," they'd say, almost in tears, "you all ain't got nothing?"

I'd tell them it was drought season. That didn't satisfy them, especially when the drought would go on for four or five days.

Just as anxious to see it end as were the dope fiends, the dealers, myself included, started going down to places like Walgreens, buying bicarbonate of soda and passing it off as coke. I'd put a little bicarbonate on a tablespoon, pour water on it, and burn it over the stove until it bubbled. When it dried up and hardened I'd scrape it off the spoon and put it in the bag. It has the same color as crack cocaine. I guess it has the same kind of hit if you smoke it. I know it does something to the crackheads. That's what they used to tell me.

If they questioned me about the quality of the phony crack, I'd tell them, "Sorry, man, that shit is whacked, a bad shipment, but I'm going to take care of you the next time."

They bought my explanation. What choice did they have if they wanted their supply to continue?

I myself never took coke, never even tried it.

To me, Rule No. 1 was, never get high off your own supply. I can't sell this stuff if I'm doing it. How was I going to make money if I kept dipping into my supply? At some point, it's going to catch up with you. I always understood that.

Junebug, like every successful drug dealer, lived by the same rule. "I was never addicted to drugs," he would tell me. "I was addicted to money."

By the time I was fifteen, a lot of my friends had added pills to their list of addictions. They would take anything in the medicine cabinet to get a super buzz and feel woozy.

I was never into that lifestyle. I tried weed a few times, but I wasn't a weedhead.

I sold. That was my thing.

Being the front man, however, was never my thing. Eventually, I hooked up with a guy on the south side who had a straight line to a well-connected source similar to the guys Junebug used from Chicago and Milwaukee, and I started getting my drugs from the new guy.

Once I established myself as an independent drug dealer, I brought in buddies like Black Rob, Li'l Greg, Mario (Tae-Tae), and Andre (Dre) to form a drug operation of my own, a junior version of Junebug's unit. After that, much like Junebug, I was never the face out there purchasing the drugs myself. After we gathered the necessary money, I would send one of the others out to make the exchange. We would meet back at the house, divide up the drugs, hit the streets, and start hustling. Some like Tae-Tae were happy sitting on a corner and selling $20 bags all day long. Others preferred the heavier stuff.

In addition to selling my share, I also directed the whole operation. I felt I was qualified to do so because, having pushed drugs since I was eleven, I had a good feel for the streets, for the dope fiends, and for the competition from other dealers. I knew who was selling weight, who was selling bags, and who was selling weed. I knew who was selling everything.

There were no secrets in the neighborhood. If a guy was unemployed and getting welfare and food stamps, yet was driving around in a Jaguar with rims on it, no one had to ask how the hell he got that. He was one of us, living off the addicts.

As good as the drug trade was for me, it got even better when a new guy set up an operation in the alley behind his house on Center Street. It was a south side version of McDonald's, a drug drive-thru. It was amazing to see long lines of cars all the way down the alley all the time, waiting to have their order filled, just like a fast-food restaurant. Everything but the golden arches.

Because I got along well with him, the new guy gave me and my little group—Black Rob and all the rest—access to that alley. That's when we started making real money. Instead of just standing on street corners, we had steady traffic, rush hour 24/7 for the serious addicts.

There were a lot of familiar faces in those long lines, and they were always bringing new faces.

We worked there all day long. Nothing stopped us.

Looking back, though, I realize with regret how oblivious I was to the damage I was doing to that neighborhood. Yes, I was just a kid caught up in making money. I was hustling, selling drugs, but I didn't see the consequences of my activities. Doing crack took days, months, years off the lives of my customers.

I didn't see the rage caused by the drugs they were taking, the highs and lows, the devastating effect of the product I put in their shaking hands. I didn't see any of that.

All I knew was, I got a lot of money and all I wanted was to get more drugs, sell more, and make even more money.

I didn't understand what I understand now. I didn't see it as a cut-throat business. To me, it was just a game. You go out there, you sell the drugs, you get rich.

What could be wrong with that?

SIX

MY LIFE ON THE STREETS: DEATH AT EVERY CORNER

In Racine's Dr. John Bryant Community Center where I first started playing organized basketball, there is a a glass display case with pictures of twenty-one black men, all under the age of twenty-five. I ran the streets with many of those guys.

Now, they are all dead.

The Racine gang wars of the 1990s, largely fueled by the drug trade, took many lives. The reason I survived was mostly luck.

There were many gangs roaming my hometown in those days like the Gangster Disciples, the Vice Lords, Land Kings, CVL, and Four Corner Hustlers.

My family was in the Gangster Disciples, or simply G.D.s as we called them. Sometimes we called ourselves the South Side Boys or SSB.

The Vice Lords was our big rival gang. Our colors were blue and black. They wore red.

My involvement in the gang life happened rather quickly once I started hustling drugs. When I was just a newspaper carrier, I was a good boy. But then, I got those crumbs of coke, I started dealing, I began making real money, and I bought the gun. All of a sudden, I had a lot in common with a crowd that had once seemed so menacing and distant to me. I was rolling with what the Disciples were rolling with. So, I was G.D. as well. We were all together.

Getting out of my house to prowl the neighborhood was easy. My kid brother, Melvin Jr., and I slept in bunk beds in a room that faced our street. All I had to do was make sure my brother was asleep, open my window, and I could step out on our big front porch to take off.

That is, assuming my mother wasn't standing there with her arms folded, shaking her head. Prison guards were easier to fool than she was. She would stick her head in my bedroom every hour until about 11:00 p.m. to check up on my brother and me.

So I would wait until midnight, arrange my pillows under the sheets to simulate my body, and then jump out of the window.

My mother's bedroom was down the hall, so she couldn't hear my comings and goings after she was tucked in for the night. Once she started working three different jobs and had all sorts of crazy shifts, sometimes coming in late at night, sometimes gone all night, sometimes up at 4:00 or 5:00 a.m., I just had to know her schedule and make sure I didn't bump into her on the porch on my way out.

Between my drug dealing and running with the wrong crowd, I missed a lot of school.

Fearing I'd get kicked out, but not wanting to let my mother know what I was up to, I went upstairs and appealed to my Aunt Kathy for help. We struck a deal. She would call the school on my behalf when parental interference was needed, or come to school and talk to my teachers and counselors. In return, I was always there for her when she needed a babysitter for her three kids.

While I was stubborn in those days, refusing to heed my mother's warnings about the dangers of the street life, I was grateful for her concern and for the love that motivated her. She had one eye on me whenever possible, even as I reached my early teens, because she understood the environment in which we lived, and realized what I was being exposed to and the effect it would inevitably have on me. After all, her older brother, Richard, was in and out of prison for selling drugs all through my formative years. So she remained super hard on me and ran me off the streets whenever possible.

Ultimately, though, the streets won.

The first really bad situation I got caught in occurred one afternoon when I was twelve. I was shooting dice with friends in an alley directly behind Noars, a corner store on Mead Street. There was also a basketball rim hanging in that alley, so my friends and I hung out there for hours, day after day, alternating between dice and hoops.

There are now concrete barriers on the section of Mead that runs by Noars to keep vehicles out, a response to the many drive-by shootings that occurred there when I was a kid. But not back then.

The possibility of a drive-by was on the minds of all us around 4:00 or 5:00 that afternoon when a white Cutlass loaded with guys came racing down Mead.

"Who dem niggers?" yelled Black Rob.

"Shit, I ain't never seen them mother fuckers before," said someone else.

The car didn't have any license plates on it, always a red flag in a rough neighborhood.

The Cutlass sped by and disappeared around a corner with its brakes screeching, so we went back to our dice game. I trusted the older guys. If they weren't concerned, neither was I.

We should have been. A few minutes later, back came that Cutlass again, this time with guns blazing.

We all started running. They kept shooting. Boom! Boom! BOOM! Then I heard the same thing from our side. Some of the guys I was with had pulled out their own hardware.

The Cutlass skidded down the street, the driver, it seemed, on the verge of losing control of the car. But he steadied it and they disappeared again, this time to a bullet escort.

That was my first experience with a drive-by. Nobody got hit, but it scared the hell out of me.

I didn't have the gun that I'd bought with me that day. Why would I? I had only gone down there on a quiet afternoon to shoot some dice and play a little basketball. But it taught me a lesson: In our hood, there are no guarantees of a quiet afternoon.

After that incident, one of the older guys with me in the alley, anger etched on his face, told us all, "We got to have someone on the point out here. We've got to start protecting our neighborhood."

That's when things changed. Everybody started carrying guns, myself included. We were always out there strapped and ready.

Any outsiders who didn't get the memo learned about the folly of challenging us a month later. We made an example of the guys in a black deuce and a quarter (a Buick Electra) that came roaring down Mead just like the Cutlass.

We weren't going for that any more. Out came our guns and off went the ammunition. We didn't shoot to kill, but we lit their asses up. I was firing right alongside everybody else.

The deuce and a quarter careened onto the sidewalk and crashed into a row of trash cans, and a few tables and chairs, sending debris and one of the car's fenders flying into the street. Then, off they went, getting the hell out of there, the only real damage being to their pride as far as I knew.

We were determined to make a stand and remain resolute that rival gangs couldn't just cruise through the south side unchallenged, feeling they were free to engage in any activities they chose. We understood that, once we took that stance, it would be a permanent policy. There would be no going back.

This was our neighborhood. We had a lot of crackheads there who paid a lot of money for their dope. We were not going to let other gangs muscle in, interfere with our operation, and get a share of the market.

We put the word out: If you crossed the tracks to come into our territory, you'd better be prepared to go to war.

That was fine with some rival gangs who vowed to break down our barriers. So they came in shooting. No trash talking. No threats. They weren't interested in having yelling matches. That was fine with us. We were ready.

As a result, there were a lot of shootouts. We fired away at any rival gang members who came through our area. Soon, they got smarter. Instead of just speeding down the main streets of Racine, guns blazing, leaving themselves open to ambushes at every corner, they would park a few blocks away, come in on foot, and try to pick some of us off. But when we heard gunshots, we'd take cover and wait for them. For a while, it was like that around the clock. You could never be without your gun, never relax, never take your eyes off the street.

I wasn't afraid of living like that, because violence and the specter of death had been a part of my life long before I started carrying a gun.

The first murder I was aware of came before I even turned eleven. The older brother of one of my future gang members killed a guy named Lazon over a dice game. Lazon, a big dude, was the guy's best friend. But when they got into an argument over a dice game, the guy pulled out a gun and shot Lazon.

When I was in the sixth grade, Tina Turner (not *that* Tina Turner), the mother of my next-door neighbor, Kiki Turner, was murdered in our neighborhood by some people who lived across the street. I saw her body on my way to school, laying in an alley unattended.

That really bothered me because this was someone I knew, but what could I do other than shrug my young shoulders. That was just the way things were on the south side.

By the time I was hanging around with the G.D.s, the Duke Hamilton Park at 18th and Mead was the center of activity on the south side, both good and bad.

Commonly referred to as the 18th Street park, it was the place where everyone hung out, the main social gathering spot. There were swing sets, a water fountain, and concrete stoops. Everybody would sit around, play cards, toss a ball, or just talk. Guys would park their cars, open their doors and windows, and blast their music on their high-tech sound systems.

In the summer, people would buy ice cream or shakes at the nearby Dairy Queen, and pause at the park to finish them.

At first glance, a visitor to our town might think this was an isle of peace and tranquility in the midst of a troubled city. And for a while, it was.

But as the drug wars intensified in Racine and the number of weapons multiplied rapidly, the violence soon spread to the 18th Street park until it became ground zero for the town's deadly explosion of violence. The word soon spread that people entering the park were putting their lives on the line, but still they came, many involved in drug dealing and the almost nightly shootouts.

The level of crime and violence in the park was not surprising considering Li'l Greg, Tae-Tae, and I along with many of the other kids dealing drugs on the south side all lived within a two-block radius of the park.

It was a weird environment. Every time I went out there, I was playing Russian roulette. Now, thinking about it as an adult, I realize how crazy it was. But, as a kid, that's all I knew. I didn't realize how much danger I was in.

Just standing in that park, I had to worry about three potential threats that could strike me at any moment. There were the rival gang members, who wouldn't hesitate to shoot me, muggers, who were always looking for opportunities to rob a young drug dealer like me, most likely loaded with cash, and the police, who were anxious to catch me in the act of dealing.

By the time I was twelve, my mother was well aware that I hung out in the 18th Street park. She knew that my friends and I drank there, smoked cigarettes and marijuana, played cards, shot dice, did all the things we thought our parents didn't know we were doing.

Other than the pot, she may have grudgingly accepted my activities as part of the growing process of a young boy, but when the violence became rampant in the park, when she could hear gunshots echoing from there all the way to our house a block and a half away, she decided to take action and put herself in the line of fire if necessary, even if that embarrassed me. From then on, when my mother thought I was at the park, or heard there had been a shooting on the park's property, she would gather a couple of her sisters, pile them into her station wagon, race to the park, and try to get me out of there.

If my friends saw her barreling down the street, they would yell, "Your mom's comin'. Your mom's comin'."

That enabled me to get out of sight, but my mother could be tricky. If I disappeared, she would turn the car around and appear to be going back home. But she'd move slowly, looking in her rearview mirror. And if I came out of hiding, she would spot me, kick the car into reverse, race backwards, and nail me.

"Why are you chasing me?" I would yell at her and my aunties when they found me. "I didn't get shot. It was someone else."

That was my argument, my thought process as a kid.

"You are out here. You could get killed," my mom would say. "Bullets don't have names on them."

"It wasn't my gun. I don't even have a gun. It was his gun," I would insist, pointing to one of my friends.

"He's your best friend," my mom would reply, "and you were with him. Now get in this car!"

She didn't just worry about me. She would tell all my friends, "You all get out of this park, too." She figured, if their parents were working, she would take responsibility for their safety as well.

My mom wound up coming down to that park every day, or at least every other day. On the way home, she would always tell me, "You're my baby and I want you to be safe."

My mom tried everything to keep me home as much as possible. She stocked the refrigerator with everything from Kool-Aid and milk to Popsicles for me and my friends. She put a rug down in the basement, and added a TV and an Atari console complete with sixty video games.

I spent a lot of time down there, but sooner or later, I would get the itch to go to the park.

My mom didn't know I was selling drugs, but she felt certain my friends and I were doing something wrong. She just couldn't figure out what it was.

My claim that I didn't have a gun was so convincing that she believed me. The truth is, I was involved in a lot of shootings at the park. Fortunately, I never caught a bullet there, but my Uncle Carlos was hit by two of them. In the days before cell phones, he was on one of the park's pay phones with his friend Jason standing beside him. Some guys came through on a drive-by and hit Uncle Carlos twice, one bullet grazing his face, the other hitting him in the back, but he survived.

Crime was rampant in Racine from the mid 1980s to the late '90s. From 1990 to 1996, we were the murder capital of Wisconsin with young people like myself being the hardest hit. Over that span, fifty-three people under the age of thirty were killed. In 1994 alone, eighteen people under the age of thirty were murdered.

In comparison, in 2013, there was one homicide in Racine in the entire year, the lowest number in thirty years. Back when I grew up, we'd have a homicide a week.

The spike in crime was triggered by a recession that hit our area especially hard at the start of the 1980s, around the time I came into this world.

Until then, the lucrative job market that had brought my family north from Mississippi had also provided stability and security for thousands of other families. Along with J. I. Case, where so many Butlers worked, and S. C. Johnson Wax, companies like Jacobsen Manufacturing, producers of lawn mowers and other gardening equipment, and Massey Ferguson, known for its tractors, were major employers in our city and the surrounding area.

The recession changed all that. Plants were closing, workers were being laid off, and opportunities were disappearing. The doors that had been open to their parents were slammed shut for the next generation. Until the '80s, kids were expected to at least get through high school and then get a job in one of Racine's many manufacturing plants. But when the economic hard times hit, the days of coming up from Mississippi and quickly landing a well-paying spot on an assembly line were over. That's why my mother had to work so many jobs and so many hours just to survive.

Also in the early '80s, the crack epidemic took off on the West Coast, especially in California. It took a few years for it to spread to the Midwest, but once it did, it struck Racine like a tornado.

As a result, kids, whose biggest crimes had been writing graffiti on garages and getting into fistfights, were suddenly entrepreneurs in an underground economy, making more money in the drug trade than their parents had ever dreamed of.

Richard Polzin, then Racine's chief of police, had only 211 policemen at the time to deal with the crime wave ravaging a population of around eighty thousand. So he figured the best strategy would be a policy of aggressiveness. He may not have had the number of police officers he would have liked, but he felt he could compensate for that by recruiting people who were dedicated, tireless, and resourceful.

Polzin and his officers decided to attack the source of much of the crime in Racine, the drug trade. Their chief weapon in this fight was the search warrant. Whenever they discovered a spot they suspected was a sanctuary for drug dealers, they quickly sought out a judge and were soon on the streets, warrant in hand.

The drug dealers also had a strategy. "Okay," they said, "the police department can't get a search warrant on this whole park."

Besides, by then, most dealers were selling crack cocaine and many buyers were smoking it in their cars around the park.

So the 18th Street park became the south side's open-air drug den. We used to call it the Highway to Heaven. So much money used to come through that park that you could throw a bag of crack out there and get rich.

No policeman was going to walk in there alone. It would be like walking onto a target range with a bull's-eye on your back. By the time the cops had gathered enough officers for a posse, we had sufficient warning to escape to the surrounding alleys where we dumped our dope. I don't think any drug dealer ever got caught in that park. It was a great environment if you were a drug dealer. Not such a great environment if you were a resident of the surrounding houses.

Frustrated, Polzin and his officers came up with a new plan. From scratch, they built an $80,000 house right there on a corner of the park and installed cameras in the windows and on the roof to monitor everyone who passed by and everything they did.

The residents loved it. They didn't have a lot of money. Most of the homes in that area were worth $10,000 to $15,000, but at least they finally had peace, quiet, and the comfort of knowing their kids would be safe laughing, running, and playing.

The park had been reclaimed from the criminals, and remains largely a safe haven for families to this day.

Sometimes people look at the inner city as a cesspool of drug dealing, dope smoking, and welfare-absorbing people. But the reality is, even during that era of peak gang violence, Racine was just like the rest of America. Eighty percent of the families owned their own home and had a traditional structure with a mother and a father in the house.

Of course, there is always going to be some criminal element in the population and, in the case of Racine, what remains today of that element has largely relocated to Mt. Pleasant, six miles west of Racine. Law enforcement officers there are now using a strategy similar to the one that cleared out the 18th Street park by building a substation of their own.

The battle goes on.

My friends and I ended up getting a car of our own, a Malibu, when I was just twelve and a half years old. Black Rob, Li'l Greg, Tae-Tae, and Dre were all involved, but because Black Rob and I sold the most drugs, made the most money, and paid for the car, we pretty much owned it. We designated Tae-Tae to be the driver. Black Rob and I were the gun-toters in the group.

We spent $800 for the car and another chunk of money to put in a sound system that same day. We'd ride around loudly blaring the sounds of N.W.A. and other groups.

One night, I borrowed my mother's Isley Brothers cassette tape and popped it into the player as we rolled down the street. With Tae-Tae behind the wheel, we pulled up at a red light. We were rocking the car pretty good from side to side to the beat of the music when Tae-Tae looked in his rearview mirror and saw two cops stopped four cars back.

"Man, police behind us!" he yelled.

Looking around frantically, we all started screaming at him to turn down the music. We were so nervous because we were carrying drugs and had no license plates on our car. Not too clever, but we were just foolish kids, none of us even in our teens.

As long as there were a couple of cars stopped between us and the cops, we were shielded. But if those cars started to peel off, we were dead.

One car behind us turned, then another.

That's when Tae-Tae panicked. He wasn't a good driver even under the best of circumstances, and this was hardly that.

He tried to make a smooth, but quick turn. Instead, he hit the gas hard, then the brakes, throwing us all forward violently.

It unraveled quickly after that. We hit the curb, drove up on the sidewalk, and kept going, straight toward the brick wall surrounding the S. C. Johnson Wax building. We smashed right through that wall before stopping, bricks flying in the air, some of them crashing down on our car and smashing the windshield.

There we sat for an instant, stunned, the Malibu half in and half out of the wall.

When the police swung around and shined a big spotlight on our car, it snapped us out of our collective daze. We fell all over each other trying to get out of the vehicle while making sure we didn't leave any telltale drugs behind.

We all made it, but then, a frightening realization hit me.

"Damn," I thought, "I've got to get my mother's cassette tape out of there. There's fingerprints on it."

So while everybody else scrambled in all directions, I turned around, leaned back in the car, thankful that I had long arms, got the tape out of the cassette player by the length of my fingertips, and took off again.

We ran through alleys, hopped over fences, and ducked into garages. The cops stuck with us for a while, but in the dark of the night, with the home-court advantage of knowing every slab of concrete and every sheltering tree in a neighborhood we'd traveled since we started walking, we were not going to be caught.

Eventually, we all met up at Li'l Greg's house, put on some of his old clothes so we wouldn't be identified when we went back out, and then sat around in his place laughing about the whole thing even though we had lost our car.

I wasn't laughing, though, when I got home and my mother confronted me. It turned out that she had driven by that spot after we had escaped. As she rolled slowly past the scene, seeing the blinking red lights of a fleet of cop cars and the old Malibu half buried under a pile of bricks, something in her heart told her I had something to do with that car even though she didn't know I had bought it.

I couldn't look her in the face and lie. I just couldn't. So I admitted everything, saying, "Yes, mom, that was my car. We got in an accident. We got chased by the police. Stuff happened."

As expected, she launched into a big lecture. "You are screwing up," she said. She told me I had to stay away from the crowd I was hanging with, stay out of the bad neighborhood, stay in school, stay on the right path.

My mom didn't say anything I hadn't heard dozens of times before, but this time, I really listened.

Even after I went to my room, I kept thinking about her words, about how close I had come to really ruining my life by putting myself in a really bad situation. I could have been arrested for having drugs on me. I could have been seriously injured in the car accident. And by running from armed policemen, I could have been shot.

It was the culmination of a couple of years of bad behavior. From the age of eleven to thirteen, it seemed like I had a regular seat in the courtroom. I spent more time there than a lot of lawyers. At one point, I was facing charges in twelve different cases at the same time. There was a lot of shit I got caught up in. It was bad.

I was on probation at the time of the car accident for an assault and battery charge after being part of a gang that jumped a kid at the Bryant Center. There had been other assault and battery charges against me, possession of firearms, reckless behavior, stealing bikes, and habitual absence from school. I had already been in several shootouts, bullets whizzing around my head while I fired back until I'd emptied my gun.

My poor mom was always trying to defend me in court, always pleading for lenience in front of a judge. They all knew her on a first-name basis.

She dealt with so many legal ramifications, I think she learned enough to have passed the bar and become a lawyer herself.

When my friends and I were out on the streets, we were always on the lookout for the rap van. Similar in appearance to a FedEx truck, the rap van was used by the Racine Police Department for raids.

When we spotted it in the neighborhood, we knew the area was about to be flooded with cops. It didn't take a lot of effort to find that van because the cops made no attempt to hide it. The words "Racine Police Department" were clearly displayed on the sides. The idea was not to go undercover in order to catch us doing something wrong, but rather to run us off the street through intimidation before we could do anything wrong.

The operation was run by a cop named Dave Boldus, a gang division police officer, and he usually had the two Kurts with him, Big Kurt and Little Kurt. Little Kurt was the meaner of the two, a guy with a crew cut and a military look. When we saw the three of them, we knew the rap van was close behind and they were about to shut down our section of the neighborhood. We were under siege.

The cops would pull up and jump out of the van. That's how they got the name "jump-out boys." But we were like roaches. By the time their boots hit the pavement, we had scattered in every direction.

We didn't all get away. They would manage to round up a few of us, order us to put our hands up, search us, ask us questions, and take our names. They knew we were up to no good.

If they charged me and I had to go to court, sometimes I got lucky because the arresting officer got lazy and didn't check my records. When that happened, I just didn't show up in court. Hell no, because it seemed like I was always dodging some arrest warrant that was out for me or on probation in another matter. And my legal status in those prior cases would have been discovered if I had walked into the courtroom.

Many times, I was stopped simply because, already close to my current height of 6'7" by the time I was thirteen, I towered over my friends and could be spotted by police a block away.

If shots were fired and I was in the neighborhood, I got questioned and often got charged.

The cops would say to me, "Come on, man, that was you. You are tall as shit. There was a shooting. We know you were there. The description was a male, over 6-foot-5 with a doo-rag and chain, just what you are wearing. Whether or not you had anything to do with it, we know you were there. If you help us, we'll let you go. So who was out there with you?"

I wouldn't answer.

"Alright," they'd tell me, "then you can sit your ass in jail."

Then I'd have another case to fight in court. It was always something.

Many times, the police would put me in the Scared Straight program. They would walk me through their jail facility and tell me, "This is where you are going to wind up."

The guards had already bribed the inmates to get them to scare us. "We'll give you all a case of sodas when they leave," the inmates would be told, "if you make this experience frightening for them."

So, as we walked down the cellblock, a bunch of inmates would poke their heads through the bars of their cells and yell out, "You don't want to be here! Don't you ever come back here!"

I'd look at them and tell them to "Fuck off." I wasn't afraid. I knew half the dudes in there.

A judge even sent me to anger-management classes. I didn't have an anger problem. I had an attitude problem. My mom had hoped her lecture had changed that attitude, but once I got back on the streets, I quickly reverted to my old habits.

Missing the freedom of having wheels after we lost the Malibu, I started driving a sky-blue Eagle that belonged to Junebug. When I say sky blue, I don't mean it was sharp looking. Far from it. The car was beat up and made a loud, ugly sound when it started up, as if it was ready for the junkyard.

Merely starting it up could be a challenge, but not for me. It was like many of today's modern cars that start up with the push of a button as long as the driver has the key on him. That's the way that old Eagle was, but not by design. The key had been lost, but if you knew how to turn the ignition switch a certain way, you could get it going.

When he was young, Junebug would often use a moped to conduct his drug business. It was the best way to get in and out of neighborhoods without drawing the attention of the cops. But then he bought the Eagle and used it to store his dope and go on drug runs. Once the big money poured into his coffers, however, he abandoned that car for newer, faster, high-end vehicles. So it just sat around rusting until my buddies and I started using it to cruise or make drug runs to the 18th Street park.

To us, it was a trap car like so many others in our neighborhood. That meant, if the police pop up driving behind you, your car becomes a garbage disposal. You can just throw it away. You jump out while it's still moving and the cops have to worry about stopping it before it crashes into something or somebody, instead of chasing you. When we were in that car, knowing we might have to ditch it, we'd say we were on "a ghost ride."

One good feature of the car was its license plates. Yes, it actually had them, in contrast to so many other vehicles around the south side. I don't know under whose name the car was registered, but those plates often caused the cops to look elsewhere for someone to pull over. After all, they had a fleet of plateless cars to choose from.

Once in a while, they still pulled me over, and then I was in trouble because I didn't have a driver's license. Not surprising since I was only thirteen.

Sometimes, instead of taking me in, they would put me in the back of their squad car and talk to me as they continued to drive around on patrol. It didn't matter if the cops were black or white. The message was always the same: "Get off these streets before something happens to you. Don't stay out here."

Two cops in particular, Treva and Dre (Andre), were always in my face, trying to reform me. I felt they honestly cared about me and didn't think they were investing their time in vain. I have since heard from others that they saw something in me that caused them to tell fellow officers, "We wouldn't be driving around with this kid, talking to him, if we thought he was just some thug. He is worth your time."

But, back then, I didn't give a damn. I didn't answer back as they spoke from the front of the patrol car, but I was thinking, "Man, you all hating on me because I'm getting all this money. I'm thirteen years old with nearly $10,000 put away, nice chains around my neck, nice clothes on my back, new shoes on my feet, a car to drive, and a couple of pagers. I'm making a lot more money than you guys are. You're jealous, but you can't stop me."

That was my attitude.

I guess I hid it pretty well from the cops. Art Howell, who is now the police chief in Racine, but was on the gang unit when I was roaming the streets, recently told me, "You had this unbelievable maturity as it related to adults and authority figures, certainly not the norm for people of that age. Even when you were going through your juvenile delinquency phase, you were always respectful to me and other police officers. Always. You had great rapport with us, which was really weird for a young person selling drugs. You were very charismatic. That is what I found fascinating about you. Some of the kids would be disrespectful to the officers and swear at them. But whatever you were thinking, you never showed us that disposition, even when you were out there doing things you shouldn't have been doing."

The credit for that has to go to my mom. She's the one who taught me good manners.

I was openly defiant when it came to my enemies on the street. I shot at a lot of people. I didn't worry about whether or not they got hit because they didn't worry about hitting me.

I did see dead bodies in the vicinity of other shootouts, but I never heard of anybody getting killed in any shootout I was involved in. I know I never murdered anybody. If somebody got shot when we were exchanging bullets with rival gangs, but that person didn't die, then that didn't count as a serious offense in my mind. Honestly, as long as the person wasn't dead, my conscience didn't bother me.

The first friend I lost to gunfire was James Barker Jr.

For ten days, there had been talk in the neighborhood about one of his guns, a Tommy gun, supposedly being stolen by someone he knew.

"I don't even give a fuck about the gun anymore," James told me. "It's just the fact that he stole it and I thought we were family."

I clearly remember the day he died. We had all been together at the Bryant Center shooting hoops. As I left with a bunch of friends, I looked around for James, but he was gone. My other buddies and I were in a great mood heading home, singing the lyrics to a Tupac song.

About two hours after arriving at my house, I heard James had been shot. We rushed over to his place, located upstairs in a duplex next to Noars, arriving before the ambulance pulled up. Once there, we learned that James had confronted the guy he thought had stolen the Tommy gun. Angry words turned into shaking fists. Apparently feeling he was overmatched, the guy shot James in the chest.

They picked him up and gently sat him down in a chair.

As some of James's other friends gently removed his jewelry and pulled off his shirt, the rest of us tried talking to him. "You alright?" someone asked. "You good?" someone else said.

At first, he was trying to talk, but then he started gasping for breath. Finally, he shuddered and slumped over.

James was still alive when the ambulance attendants arrived. They seemed to stabilize him, told us he was going to be okay, and then carefully carried him downstairs.

But he wasn't okay. They took him to St Luke's Memorial Hospital and then transferred him to St. Mary's Hospital.

That's where James died. He was just sixteen.

I thought, "I was just with him. How the hell did this happen?"

Until they are directly involved, people don't see the consequences of what bullets do, don't know the number of lives they can affect. James's shooter ended up getting thirty to forty years in prison. It was sad because it was all over nothing really. Just a gun. That was crazy.

It was my first true dose of reality. That murder really put everything in perspective. I saw the street life differently for the first time.

I realized, when you shoot at somebody, you make that person feel like he needs to be a shooter, too. Maybe you create a killer. When he comes back through your neighborhood, he's definitely looking to hurt somebody. There's a domino effect.

You don't see all those things when you are in the middle of it. You need to step away to get a clear view of what the hell is going on in your violent world.

When you go to as many funerals as I did, the message is pounded into your brain that this is no way to live if you want to keep on living. And it wasn't just me. In our neighborhood, when somebody died, it touched everybody, the whole city, north side, south side, midtown. It's not like these people were living in some distant city and I was only learning about their deaths through the media. It was all right there in Racine, so close to home. The funeral processions resulting from the gang wars traveled through every neighborhood to get to the graveyard.

Everybody saw them. Everybody was impacted.

As the murders piled up after we lost James, dudes that I ran with, just saw on a regular basis or bumped into in stores, alleys, or the park, weren't around anymore. I no longer saw their smiles, heard their laughs, listened to them cracking jokes, banged up against them while hooping at the Bryant Center. They were no longer a part of my daily routine.

Death was all around me. Guys were killing dope fiends, shooting them and then leaving them dead in cars or the gutters. The bodies of neighbors who had habitually been under the influence could be seen up and down the alleys around my house, their final moments of agony still etched on their faces.

I felt empty. I thought, "This shit is real. This death thing is getting contagious. People are not coming back from it."

My mother's lecture may have gotten my attention, but it was the sounds of silence that validated her words.

It started changing me. Not suddenly, but gradually. It's not easy changing ideas that have been ingrained in you since you first started figuring things out. I had lived my entire young life in a crime-ridden ghetto thinking there was no honest way out.

A lot of my friends stayed stuck in that same mind-set, still doing the same dangerous, reckless stuff they had always done.

But not me. I knew I needed to slow down, chill, think about my future more. I started living differently, thinking differently, pulling further and further away from my old lifestyle.

When I saw all those dead bodies, I realized how easily that could have been me. Or could have easily been me killing somebody else. Once you put yourself in that situation and somebody forces your hand, you are not going to back down.

I didn't want to be in that situation anymore.

SEVEN

MY UNCLES: SURVIVORS FROM THE SOUTH SIDE

Even though he was in prison, my Uncle Carlos heard about my exploits with guns and drugs.

He called me one day from the penitentiary and asked, "What the fuck you doing out there?"

"Just trying to make a little money," I told him.

It felt good to know he was still trying to watch out for me.

I often felt alone in those days because my two uncles, Carlos and Richard, were gone for long stretches of time, locked up behind bars. I had my grandmother and my mother and my four aunts, but for all my big talk, I still needed a male presence in my life, someone who had taken the same road I was traveling and could warn me about the hazards up ahead. I looked up to both my uncles. They were the dudes who used to take me under their wings and try to keep me on a straight path. Without them, I felt nobody had my back, nobody was there to steer me right if I took a wrong turn.

Uncle Richard, my grandmother's firstborn, was the first to get into the drug trade.

Before that—out of school and out of his teens—he had been working at the Bryant Center as a janitor. The thing was, Uncle Richard's salary was barely enough to survive, and he had child support payments and a string of unpaid traffic tickets. All he could see in his future was a jail cell.

His friends saw a way out, ironically one that could also land him in a jail cell. They were always whispering in his ear that working a regular job led to a dead end. Drug dealing led to unimaginable riches. It wasn't just talk to him. He saw the fast cars they drove, the hip clothes they wore, the high-end shoes that propelled them down the hardwood.

Uncle Richard had "dipped and dabbed," as he put it, in drug dealing as a teenager, but always pulled back, determined not to disappoint his mother, my grandmother.

But by the time he had turned twenty-one, he felt he was falling into a financial abyss from which there was no escape, and was tired of constantly asking for handouts from those around him. Instead, Uncle Richard quit working at the Bryant Center and became a full-time drug peddler.

"I decided I was going to do whatever I had to do to get money to pay the bills," he once told me. "I didn't have anybody reliable I could count on, so I counted on myself."

It seemed like a great move at first. Uncle Richard was in a group that sold ten kilos of crack cocaine a week, worth about $250,000. Even though it had to be divided twenty ways, that still gave him $12,500. He soon bumped that up, pocketing $25,000 to $30,000 a week.

That's when he got the nickname Daddy Rich.

Uncle Richard hid the money from his mother, determined to keep her from learning what he had become. He also hid it from me.

But while he may have concealed the mountains of money he was amassing, he wasn't stingy with it. He would slip cash to his sisters and me all the time and always surprise us with gifts.

"I worried a lot about setting a bad example for you," he told me. "I didn't want to be anybody's role model. I was just doing what I had to do."

For Uncle Richard, the corner hustler was his role model.

Even though he didn't want to be my role model, he was just that. He was a Gangster Disciple before I was.

"I wasn't a shooter," he told me. "If I didn't like someone, I'd fight them. I didn't want to kill people. I just wanted them to leave me alone."

Like me, Uncle Richard never used drugs. But, he said, "I sold the hell out of them. It was fun while I was doing it, but when I got caught, it was horrible."

Uncle Richard got caught over and over again, but he kept coming back for more.

"First time I went to prison," he said, "I was twenty-two. I served a year before getting out. That wasn't enough.

"I was convicted in another drug case and went back to prison, that time for three years. That wasn't enough.

"Again I got caught in a drug deal, again I went to prison, serving six years, double my previous sentence. That wasn't enough."

Ultimately I played a role in getting Uncle Richard to finally admit that enough was enough.

Sitting at home in Racine one night in front of his TV, he was watching me play for the Washington Wizards. When the game ended, the lead story on the local news that followed was about one of the biggest drug busts ever in the area. And there on the screen as the details were announced was a photo of Uncle Richard. He was one of those who had been indicted.

The connection was obvious. He had been highlighted because he was related to me and everybody in Racine knew who I was.

"Something died in me that night," Uncle Richard later told me, "because I didn't want to hurt my family and I realized that's what I was doing.

"Everybody knew I had a famous nephew who had millions of dollars, who always gave me what I wanted, but I still wanted to sell drugs."

Sitting in a five-by-nine cell for seventeen days while waiting to go before a judge, Uncle Richard prayed, promising that, if he got out, he would never do anything that would put him back in that situation again.

He got probation rather than jail time.

"I lucked out," he said.

That changed Uncle Richard. He reevaluated his life, finally got off the streets, and went to work for one of my aunts, who, backed by the money I've put into family businesses, owns several group homes. Uncle

Richard works there with the disabled and the elderly. He also works for a Racine YMCA.

It's been six years since his transformation and he hasn't been back to jail since.

"That's really good for me," he said. "I finally caught on."

But the itch has never gone away, even though Uncle Richard doesn't scratch it.

"Even though I have a nephew who has been in the NBA for thirteen years," he says now, "I still have this thing in the back of my head that I can sell drugs. It has nothing to do with Caron. I don't think he understands that I still have to be a man. He has his life. I have to have my own life. He's always telling me that I don't have to do this, but I was always my own provider. I do for me. So yes, it was very hard to give it up."

Uncle Richard only needs to look at most of the other members of the crowd he ran with to know that he has done the right thing.

"Mostly all my buddies I hung out with are dead and gone," he says. "I got a couple of buddies still around. One of them went to prison two years ago for drug dealing. They gave him ten years. That shook me up. He's fiftysomething years old. When he gets out, he'll be sixtysomething. What will he have when he's been gone for so long? It's not like when you went to prison when you were eighteen and got out when you were twenty-nine. You can't get any retirement benefits because you've never worked a job. It's hard."

Uncle Richard deeply appreciates the fact that he can walk around free every day.

"I feel lucky," he says. "Whoever prayed for me, I thank them. I know my still being here came from prayers. I was in the streets, not caring what I had to go through to get money. I was out of control, but I never hurt anybody. I'm very blessed because it all turned out for the best."

Uncle Carlos was different. When he went to the Bryant Center, it was to play hoops. And he was a great player. When he thought about his future, he was confident it would include basketball, not drug dealing.

Just four when he started playing, first in pickup games and then in age-group leagues, Uncle Carlos always wound up with the older kids. He was dominant among those his own age. The only way to challenge him was to put him on the court with the bigger kids.

At ten, he was asked to join an AAU team. By the time he reached high school, he was a polished player, a 6'2" guard who could really shoot the ball well.

He was the star of the family, not me.

And the court wasn't the only place Uncle Carlos excelled at J. I. Case High School. He did extremely well in the classroom, so much so that he was being considered for an academic scholarship at Northwestern University. Sure, it was his skill on the basketball court that got the attention of the Northwestern recruiters, but when they saw his grades, they realized they would be getting double the return on their investment.

Uncle Carlos assured the staff at Northwestern that would be the case. "I'm not just an athlete," he told them. "I'm a student-athlete."

My family and I had invested our hopes in his potential on the court. After all, we had been coming to his games and cheering him on since his AAU days. But we weren't there when he devoted his private hours to reading the *New York Times*, *Chicago Tribune*, and *Time* magazine. We didn't see him studying the business section of those publications, teaching himself the inner workings of the stock market and generally focusing on economics.

"I never wanted to be what everybody else wanted me to be," Uncle Carlos told me. "In my head, I wanted to be something other than an athlete. But if I had to use basketball to get to where I wanted to be, so be it."

We'll never know what he would have become if he had been allowed to reach his full potential, either on or off the court. But back then, he was poised to become the first Butler to go to college.

If only Uncle Carlos hadn't hung around with the wrong crowd. Of course, you didn't have much choice if you grew up on the south side.

He took me everywhere with him until his friends started selling drugs. Then suddenly, one day, he told me, "You can't come around no more, I don't need you to see the stuff they are doing." I was kind of hurt, but I understood.

Uncle Carlos didn't see it as a problem for himself. He enjoyed the company. Most of his friends were guys he had known since he was a toddler at the Bryant Center. And he had his self-imposed limits. He drew the line at drugs. He didn't use them, didn't sell them, didn't carry them, didn't even touch them.

He saw what was happening around him, and he was determined to live a better life. So after he roamed the streets with his friends, he would come home and do his homework.

Uncle Carlos was committed to making sure I lived a better life as well. When I first started dealing drugs, I tried my best to hide my activities from him because I knew how hard he would come down on me.

A couple of times, he caught me on the corner where the dealers did their business simply because he was hanging with his friends who were doing the same thing. When Uncle Carlos spotted me, he would either order me off the street, yelling, "Get away from here. The streets ain't for you." Or he would grab me by the back of my neck and point me home.

I understand why he did that. He's told me many times that I'm the little brother he never had.

When I was twelve, my secret was revealed. A friend of Uncle Carlos told him that his nephew had joined the ranks of the dealers.

Shocked, he came straight to the corner where I had just made a sale.

He was mad. And that made me mad. We went at it pretty good verbally right there on the corner. I didn't back down a bit. Nor did he.

"This is not what you want to do," Uncle Carlos told me. "This is a very demanding existence. Nobody makes it out of this lifestyle. I look at the dudes I've grown up with. Some have been killed and many others have gone to jail."

When you are the age I was at the time, you think you are bulletproof. I assured him I wasn't going to wind up a loser.

Uncle Carlos told me that, even if I survived, I wouldn't like the person I would become.

"This game changes people," he said. "The greed affects your whole mind-set. It takes over. Even if you think you'll get out at some point, the greed won't let you. It also screws up your relationship with your buddies. Jealousy messes with your judgment. Best friends turn on each other. You don't need that in your life. That's not what you want to be around. You need to stay focused on a better future."

I had stopped arguing and just listened. I think I convinced Uncle Carlos that he had made me see the error of my ways. We left that corner together and I could tell he felt good about intervening.

But he wouldn't have felt so good if he had seen what happened next.

As soon as Uncle Carlos was out of sight, I went right back to that corner.

I wish Uncle Carlos had been as concerned about hanging around drug dealers himself as he was for me. By being in the company of Junebug, someone he'd hung with since they were kids, Uncle Carlos wound up in a disastrous situation that destroyed his dreams for his future.

He knew Junebug was a drug dealer, the biggest in the city, but Uncle Carlos refused to let that ruin a life-long friendship that turned into a strong family tie when Junebug married Uncle Carlos's sister, my Aunt Kathy.

"He never put me in harm's way until that moment," explained Uncle Carlos.

That moment came when police raided a house where he and a friend of his were in the basement watching Junebug cook cocaine into crack form that would be worth around $21,000 on the street.

Uncle Carlos may have felt safe since they were in the home of one of his sisters, my Aunt Tina. But, armed with a search warrant, Officer Boldus charged into that house, followed by several other officers. They looked around, saw the opening to the basement, and raced down the stairs.

If the coke had been in powder form, Junebug, upon hearing the furious footsteps, could have dissolved the dope in water.

Instead, he had several large chunks of crack on a plate in his hand. He did the only thing he had time to do, hurling the plate across the basement floor. Both the plate and the chunks shattered into pieces.

The police had to smile. There were pieces of crack all over the floor. For the cops, it was like picking up pieces of candy. It doesn't get much sweeter than that for arresting officers.

The risks of being in the wrong place at the wrong time, whether innocent or guilty, had been made very clear by the Racine P.D. If you are in a house or a car or any other enclosed area and drugs are discovered, everybody present will be considered equally guilty unless someone comes forward and confesses to being the sole owner of the dope.

That crack belonged to Junebug. He doesn't deny that to this day. But on that day, he didn't say anything.

All three people in the room, Uncle Carlos and his friend along with Junebug, were arrested, charged, convicted, and sent to prison.

"He took us both down with him," said Uncle Carlos.

His friend barely knew Junebug.

So why would Junebug do that? Why wouldn't he just admit the drugs were his and his alone?

"You are not thinking like that at the time," he explained to me. "You figure, the more people in the house, the more arrests, the less time each of us is going to get."

I know Uncle Carlos sees it differently.

"I trusted him and he didn't do the right thing," said my uncle of Junebug. "Sometimes people don't own up to their stuff and everybody suffers."

Uncle Carlos was sentenced to ten years in prison, incarcerated in 1994 right after he graduated from high school.

He was eighteen and a half.

Not only did he wave goodbye to his family, but to Northwestern, basketball, and the dreams of all that could follow, whether that was a career in the NBA or on Wall Street.

That's why Uncle Carlos's story is so sad. Drugs had ruined another life on the south side, only this time it was someone who was innocent, but in the wrong place at the wrong time.

He moved around a lot in the Wisconsin penal system. He was in Dodge Correctional Institution in Waupun, Green Bay Correctional,

Gordon Correctional, Columbia Correctional in Portage, Fox Lake Correctional, Jackson Correctional in Black River Falls, and McNaughton Correctional in Lake Tomahawk.

Sentencing guidelines for crack cocaine were much more stringent than for powder cocaine. As a result, a lot of inner-city kids caught with crack were locked up for much longer periods of time. A lot of people don't think that's fair, that the policy fails to meet the standard of equal punishment under the law. I've been told by law-enforcement officials that, no matter what part of the country you look at, there has been a lot of violence, a lot of death associated with crack cocaine trafficking. And that's the rationale they use for the disparity in sentencing.

I feel good that I gave Uncle Carlos the only real enjoyment he had during those horrible years. Once I started to excel on the basketball court in high school and into my first year at UConn, he kept a scrapbook of me in action. With little else of interest in their lives, his fellow inmates loved looking through the book every time he updated it. He even left it behind for them when his prison days were over.

When he wasn't collecting articles and photos of me, mostly from newspapers, he was writing me letters, warning me not to hang with the wrong crowd. But the way I looked at it, I was doing the same thing he did.

Uncle Carlos finally got out after seven years and ten months.

He was twenty-six, free, but a lost soul.

"I was totally out of touch," he said. "Because I had been gone that long, everything had changed. The city changed, people changed, and I myself was a dramatically different person."

Not for the better. He was bitter.

"There had been peace in my soul before I went in," Uncle Carlos said, "but there was no peace when I got out because of the situation that had put me in there."

Mostly, there was hate in his soul. He trusted no one, including family members and friends. He certainly didn't trust those he considered enemies, and he saw enemies everywhere.

That left Uncle Carlos isolated. So he turned inward.

"I became a really selfish person," he admitted.

When he went to prison, Uncle Carlos had left behind two kids, a son, Carlos Jr., and a daughter, Tyra. After all those years, I know it was tough for him to reconnect with them.

"I wasn't zoned in sufficiently on getting back to fatherhood, on being there for them like I was before I left," Uncle Carlos told me. "I was so mad that I couldn't focus on what I wanted to do, what I needed to do. I wasn't being a good dad. I was too busy hating everyone."

His bitterness grew when he had to stay behind as the rest of the family traveled to New York to watch in person as I was drafted by the Heat. He was forbidden from traveling out of Racine County under the terms of his release and had to wear an electronic ankle bracelet to ensure that he abided by that restriction.

It took more than a year and a medical miracle to bring Uncle Carlos all the way back.

The year was 2003. I was about to start my second season in the NBA, playing for the Heat. Uncle Carlos, twenty-eight and still in mourning for his lost years, had just welcomed a second son, Marcus, into the world.

My wife, Andrea, and I were in the delivery room with about eighteen other family members and friends when Marcus arrived. Suddenly, we were all stunned into silence, the joy of his birth quickly replaced by the fear of his death when we all realized he had stopped breathing.

While the rest of us stood there helpless as doctors worked on Marcus, Uncle Carlos looked up and said quietly, so quietly that most of us couldn't hear him, "God, if you let him breathe, if he comes back, I'm going to change."

Within seconds, Marcus did start breathing, and from that moment on, Uncle Carlos never wavered from his vow.

A couple of months earlier, a former high school basketball opponent of his bumped into my Aunt Tina. This guy had gone on to become a hoops coach at Carthage College, a Division III school right on Lake Michigan in Kenosha, Wisconsin.

He had seen Uncle Carlos play in a couple of games in the midnight league at the George Bray Neighborhood Center in Racine and was impressed enough to make a mental note to reach out to him. When he saw my aunt, that triggered his memory and he handed her his card.

Who knows why seeing Marcus's lungs inflate reminded my aunt of her chance meeting with the coach, but that's what happened.

When things calmed down and the delivery room was again filled with joy, my aunt pulled out the card and handed it to Uncle Carlos.

I wouldn't blame him for thinking this unlikely opportunity had come straight from heaven.

"Oh, I got this card from this guy back in March," my aunt said nonchalantly.

"March?" Uncle Carlos said. "It's August."

"Just call him," she said. "If you want to go to school, he wants to talk to you about playing."

Because it was already late summer, there wasn't much time to think it over. School was going to start in three weeks.

It wasn't Northwestern, but it was a lot better than the midnight league at the Bray Center.

Uncle Carlos played at Carthage College for two years. He had to listen to the snickers from his teammates, some of whom were a decade younger than him. But once he got out on the court, there were no snickers. Nobody called him Old Man then.

After those two years, he came to DC when I started playing for the Wizards. He stayed there five years, until I moved on, and is now back at Carthage in his senior year, finishing up his pursuit of a degree in business with a minor in economics, a quest he had originally planned on beginning twenty years earlier.

Even before he graduates, he has begun applying the knowledge about business that he began collecting in high school. I've set up various businesses with money I've earned in the NBA, and Uncle Carlos has chosen to work in some of my homes for the mentally ill.

"We want to keep the money within the family," he said. "It's better than working for someone else and making them rich."

I encourage all of my family members to create their own income within the family businesses. We can all help each other make money the right way.

I'm so proud of the life Uncle Carlos is making for himself. I smile when I hear him say, "I have a lot to bring to the table. I want to pass my knowledge on to my kids, nieces, and nephews."

Does Uncle Carlos ever think about what might have been in terms of a basketball career had he not been in that house that night with Junebug?

There's no way to keep those thoughts from seeping into his head. But one thing I've never heard him do is brag about his skills on the court.

"How good was I?" Uncle Carlos says when prodded by others. "I go by what other people say. I don't like talking about myself. Not real big on myself. I'll let somebody else tell you. The most I'll say is that I was alright. I was pretty fair."

He really believed that at the time. It is only now that he hears from others about his skill level as a youngster that he appreciates the heights he might have attained.

My mother's Uncle Eugene, the first in the family to come to Racine, was also the first to tell Uncle Carlos he had real talent. "You got it," Uncle Eugene would say to him all the time.

People might discount that praise because it came from a family member. But Jameel Ghuari, who has coached generations of Racine players, myself included, and is not prone to handing out compliments, says of Uncle Carlos, "He was a pro. He had everything."

Everything but good luck.

By telling the stories of my uncles, I hope to make people more open-minded about judging others. Point out Uncle Richard and say he was in and out of prison for years, or mention Uncle Carlos and his nearly eight years in prison for drug dealing, and sympathy is not going to be the normal reaction.

But when you eliminate the stereotypes by telling how they turned their lives around, the only reaction should be admiration.

EIGHT

MY GAME: SHOOTING HOOPS, AIMING FOR THE STARS

Basketball was not my first love when it came to intense competition. It was video games.

Honestly.

I was into games with spaceships, wars of conquest, karate battles, Super Mario Bros, all of them. And I used to prefer playing the games by myself rather than against friends.

If it wasn't for Uncle Carlos, who is six years older than I am, it might have taken a lot longer before I finally got off the couch.

The only way he could drag me to the park to play ball, his first choice, was to trick me. He'd tell me he would play video games with me as long as I wished without complaining. But then, I'd have to agree to go to the park for hoops or football.

Uncle Carlos was persistent. Once we'd played a few video games, he shut them off and announced it was time to head for the park, like it or not.

I was never going to leave his side, so off I went. And once I got there, I loved it, of course.

The main attraction of sports, at first, was that Uncle Carlos was there with me. With Richard, my older uncle, gone much of the time, we lived in a house full of females with my grandmother and her five daughters, including my mom. So we, the two boys, stuck together, the wannabe men of the house.

Football was Uncle Carlos's first love, so it was my first love too. I did everything he did. Not because he told me to do so, but because I wanted to be just like him. When he became an excellent wide receiver, I studied his every move and became a pretty good wide receiver myself.

Next came basketball. Uncle Carlos had been dribbling a ball since he could walk, but it was only after he gave up football following a knee injury that he put his whole mind and body into hoops and showed he was a natural at it.

My grandmother made sure we all supported Uncle Carlos in his organized leagues, whether it was Small Fry basketball (called junior AAU back then), AAU for the older kids, or high school ball.

The way *Friday Night Lights* is with football in Texas, that's how it is with basketball in Racine. It takes on a life of its own.

All my aunties worked at Taco Bell at that time. We would meet there to go to Uncle Carlos's AAU or high school games, sit together, and have a Butler cheering section. Going with the family to watch him, starting at age six, is what ultimately turned me on to basketball.

To me, the most exciting team he was on was the AAU traveling squad coached by a guy named Rudy Collum, who had a sponsorship deal with Converse and other programs geared to inner-city kids. That team went everywhere from the Bahamas to Hawaii.

We obviously couldn't afford to fly to places like that to be with him, but just being exposed to the idea that places like that existed and he was going there opened up my world to the idea of limitless possibilities through basketball.

We did travel with him when feasible, all piling into my grandmother's deuce and a quarter, and later her Cadillac, and following Uncle Carlos's team bus.

For the first time, video games took a back seat to those wonderful trips to new towns and new courts around the Midwest, wherever his teams suited up.

When I started playing sports in elementary school, along with basketball, I liked kickball, volleyball, and, my favorite, tetherball. I was the man at that game. Or I guess, the boy, in those days. That was my thing.

Like Uncle Carlos, my mom pushed me into basketball from age five on. In her mind, every hour I spent on the court would be one less hour I spent on the street.

Whatever I was playing, from the youngest age I can remember, I wanted to win more than anybody I knew. Like the guys I've come to know at the highest levels of hoops, I was super-competitive.

But it wasn't just in sports. When I was a paperboy for the *Journal Times*, I wanted to have the most routes. If somebody had 250 houses, I wanted 300. When I sold drugs, if someone told me he was selling his bags for $20, I wanted bigger bags so I could sell them for $30.

Once I started playing basketball, I wanted to play everywhere, even at home. Since we didn't have a backyard, I decided to make a court in my room. I got a wire hanger, bent it into a circle, put it on the top of the door, and shut the door.

That was my hoop, sturdy for a while and easy to replace when it finally collapsed.

My friends and I would get a pair of socks and fold them up real tight into a knot so they wouldn't stretch out, and that was our ball.

We'd tally up the score on the wall next to the doorway, making little marks with a knife every time someone scored a basket. We'd dunk, hit jumpers, play defense, even count fouls.

As you might imagine, as time went by, those marks on the wall were everywhere from floor to ceiling. It looked like a prisoner behind bars was marking the days of his imprisonment and was up to twenty years.

Kind of prophetic, as it turned out.

When I was a kid, I rooted for players rather than teams, based on their styles, moves, ball-handling, and dunks, although I did like the Bucks because they were my hometown club.

Because everybody in the neighborhood played with those purple and gold Magic Johnson basketballs, Magic became one of my heroes, but my favorite player was Michael Jordan.

I used to get glimpses of Magic and Bird going at it on TV, but pro basketball didn't really come heavy into my life until we started getting

WGN-TV, the Chicago station that carries Bulls games. It was the mid-1980s when MJ was just coming into the league.

Right from the start, he was huge in my neighborhood, a kid like us who seemed to come out of nowhere with a story we in the inner city could relate to. He hadn't even made his varsity basketball team in high school at first, but look at what he became. He gave us hope.

I saw MJ's influence and his brand everywhere in Racine. I saw more people on the playground and in the park with a basketball in their hands because of him. It was a movement that swept me up along with so many others, growing into a cultural change.

We all pretended we were Michael. Every time someone in the neighborhood went to the basket, you'd see him stick his tongue out like MJ. Every time you'd see someone in his car drive through the neighborhood, he'd be sticking his tongue out as if to say, "I'm Michael Jordan on these streets. I'm Michael Jordan on the courts."

Like Uncle Carlos, I started playing in pickup games at the Bryant Center when I got a little older. We would take the best players from our recreation center on the south side and go up against other recreation centers, especially the main one on the north side. That was a great rivalry. We even traveled as far away as Rockford, Illinois, for a game.

At age seven, I went to my first professional game. It was at MECCA Arena in Milwaukee, the Bucks against the 76ers. The Bucks had given about fifty seats to our community center and we were all bussed up.

With the exception of a trip to Columbus, Mississippi, when I was very little, that bus ride to Milwaukee was the first time I had ever been off my own block, much less out of Racine. That's what happens when you live in a small city. You stay in your neighborhood because where else are you going to go that is any different?

I don't really count the trip to Mississippi, because I slept the whole way there. I woke up to snakes, along with chickens, roosters, and other farm animals. That's all I remember. When we took off to come back home, I fell into another deep sleep and woke up back in Racine. Not much of a trip in my mind.

Going to Milwaukee, on the other hand, seemed like a major journey. I remember we each had to bring gas money and we sat on the biggest bus I had ever been on. Even the trip itself seemed long, though it was only twenty miles, a fraction of the distance to Mississippi.

Milwaukee itself seemed like Oz compared to Racine. My friends and I were all looking out the windows, eyes wide, as we drove through town. To us, it was all amazing. Every building was bigger than the downtown courthouse that towered over Racine. Seeing so many big buildings in Milwaukee, seeing some of them glowing at night on the way home, seeing all the people and all the traffic, I was in awe.

They sat us in the nosebleed section of the arena, but I didn't care. I would have sat outside on the roof in the snow if I could have had a view of the court.

There was all sorts of stuff going on in MECCA Arena before the game even began, the vendors hawking their products, the cheerleaders dancing in their sparkling, glowing outfits. To me, it was mind-blowing. I had never had that much fun in my life.

And the players hadn't even taken the floor yet.

I can still remember Sidney Moncrief, the first one out, shooting around before the game in his green Bucks uniform. It seemed like the greenest green imaginable, like that uniform would hug your body and make you a great basketball player, even if you didn't have any skill at all.

It was exciting to me, but confusing. Pointing to the players, I said to the kid next to me, "Damn, out of all the people in the world, how the hell did *they* get on an NBA team? Is there a school of the NBA or something?"

That may sound weird, but as a kid, I didn't know how it all worked. I couldn't understand how you got from a place like the Bryant Center to the NBA. How does that happen? What separates us in our gym from these guys in this arena? How do you get to play here? I couldn't figure it out, but I thought it was the coolest shit ever.

Once the game started, I was fascinated by one of the guards who was dribbling the ball down the court. I stood up in my seat and pretended I was handling the ball just like him.

I decided, when I got home, I was going to work on all my moves so I could look like that on the court. I was going to go in my room, grab my rolled-up socks, or a tennis ball, and practice on my wire-hanger hoop.

I loved everything about that day, including the huge crowd. Ok, so there were only 11,052 fans there, but it was more people than I had ever seen in one place.

The day even had a perfect ending with Milwaukee winning, 106–103.

Two weeks after we saw the Bucks, our group again got tickets through the community center, this time to attend a Milwaukee Brewers baseball game. Again we got on the bus. I was becoming a regular traveling man.

During the game, a batter hit a foul ball in my direction. I attempted to catch it, but I didn't have a glove, and I wasn't used to the speed of a ball coming off a major-league bat. As a result, I whiffed and the ball hit me in the face, busting my lip.

I didn't care because I wound up with the ball and a hands-on experience at my first major-league game. Once more, I had been exposed to an exciting new world.

I loved it, but when that game was over, I realized it had just made me want to reach my initial goal more than ever. I still wanted to play basketball, not baseball. At the Brewers game, I hadn't seen a lot of brothers out there on the field. When I had watched the Bucks, the players on the floor seemed like older versions of myself. They were slender, lanky, and athletic. I was slender, lanky, and, being young and cocky, damn athletic in my own mind.

I thought, "I could do what those guys are doing."

In those years, I would still play a lot of kids' games, especially at the playground behind the Stephen Bull Fine Arts Elementary School. One of our favorite games was don't-touch-the-ground tag. The rules were simple. You had to go from the monkey bars to the slide or vice-versa without letting your feet touch the ground if you didn't want to become "it."

Afterward, we would play basketball. But more and more, as I turned nine, ten, eleven, we quit the kids' games early to pick up a basketball. The game was taking over my young life. I couldn't get enough of it.

We had two courts to play on, one a full court, the other a half court, the two side by side. We certainly didn't have breakaway rims on the playground, so, naturally, once in a while, a kid would hang too long on the rim and it would break.

When that happened, we would play on the parallel half courts, running sideways. It was crazy, yeah, but we did what we had to do to keep the game going.

When we first started there, there were chain nets. That was so cool. But eventually, they broke off.

In our neighborhood, if something on the playground broke, we knew it was going to be a long time, if ever, before it got fixed. Who had money to do that?

There were certainly no lights out there, but we all learned to use the dark as an advantage. The later it got, the more cheating went on. You'd take a shot, and even if it was an air ball, with the sunlight gone and night closing in, you would simply claim the shot was good.

"That went in."

"No it didn't."

"Looked to me like it went in."

We'd play in the snow as well. Sometimes, we'd find a shovel and clear a path to the basket. When there was no shovel, we'd simply dribble through the white stuff. There were times the snowfall was so heavy that the entire court disappeared, but we didn't care. As long as we could see the basket, we would keep playing.

When there was a little money coming into the house, I would convince my mom to buy gloves for me by complaining about how cold it was playing basketball out there in the snow. Some of my friends were just as convincing to their parents.

The problem was, the gloves may have kept your fingers warm, but they prevented you from getting a good feel, and certainly a good grip on the ball. So what we all wound up doing was cutting off the tips of those gloves to keep our fingers free.

That didn't go over too well when you came home. My mom, like many other parents in the neighborhood, would look at those missing tips and say, "You know how hard I had to work to pay for those gloves? We ain't got no money for you to be tearing them up."

I can't even count how many spankings I got for that.

At twelve and thirteen, I was deep into my drug dealing and gang-banging nights, but the days were still reserved for basketball. With all that some of us were doing on the wrong side of the law, the common denominator for the kids in my neighborhood was basketball. No matter what else was happening, we always met up at the Bryant Center for our free lunches. The courts, of course, were also there, so we played every day. And the older I got, the better I got, becoming one of the stars of the neighborhood.

It was only when those games and those that followed at Stephen Bull were over that my friends and I went back to doing our dumb, dangerous shit.

Sometimes we'd have to temporarily interrupt our games right in the middle when duty called. We would play at the Bryant Center from 1:00 to 3:00 in the afternoon, then head over to Stephen Bull to play from 4:00 to 6:00. But if the buzz of one of our pagers broke through the sounds of bouncing balls and squeaking sneakers, we would call a timeout, go make a drug sale, then come right back to the center or the playground and pick up where we had left off, like we'd just taken an ice cream break.

Junebug used to tease me all the time, saying I wasn't much of a player, but by the time I was ten, he didn't intimidate me anymore. Not surprising considering I was already bigger than him.

One day at Stephen Bull before I had turned eleven, he said, "Caron, you beat me one-on-one, I'll buy you some new shoes just like these," pointing to the bright, sharp Air Jordans on his feet.

"He made one move on me," Junebug later recalled, "went to the hole, and whoosh! I don't think I scored a point on him."

I sure did enjoy those Jordans. That was a big step up for me. Until then, I had only seen Air Jordans on TV, but there was no way I could afford them. So I wore Pony or Jordache shoes, brands that came about as close to Jordans as I was going to get until I stepped on the court with Junebug.

I was playing so well that some of the older cats at the Bryant Center started to pay attention to me, started to see my potential even before I did.

"Man, you need to do something with that game of yours," they would tell me. "You need to get on one of those Small Fry teams. Or get on Coach Rudy's traveling team that goes around the country. You need to get out of here so people can see you."

Just playing for Coach Rudy might have helped me down the line since he was also a basketball coach at the University of Wisconsin–Parkside in Kenosha. But back then, I never thought about the future.

As it turned out, one of the guys who worked with Coach Rudy in the Racine Parks, Recreation & Cultural Services department, a former football player named Walley Walter Rhome, had a son named Michael who was a friend of mine. With those connections and Uncle Carlos's history with Coach Rudy, I was able to get a spot on Coach Rudy's team, the Running Rebels.

I joined right after James Barker Jr. was killed, the first friend I'd seen die due to gun violence. The timing for becoming a Running Rebel was perfect. I badly needed to get away from the neighborhood for at least a little while.

Once in uniform, I proved that I deserved a place on the roster. Playing with and against kids my own age, I was a dominant force on the floor. I think that's because I had been playing against older kids in my neighborhood most of my life, and to prove I belonged, I had developed an overly aggressive and physical style.

"When you were a little kid," Uncle Richard once told me, "you stood out because you weren't scared of nothing. You were always very determined. If someone told you that you couldn't do something, you were going to prove them wrong. With most kids, when you put them in against bigger kids, they wouldn't play. But you played. You didn't care. You had the dog in you. You would play anybody. I knew then that there was something there."

With my aggressive style giving me an edge, I was soon the Butler who was a traveling basketball player, the one the family followed, just as they had done to watch Uncle Carlos before me. Until then, it had always been about him. Never about me. But all of a sudden, there I was, the new star in the family.

My first trip as a player was to Menomonee Falls in Waukesha County outside of Milwaukee.

It was amazing for a thirteen-year-old. One minute, I'm on the street selling drugs and in the local gym playing ball. Suddenly, I'm on the road in uniform, playing in new cities and new gyms, just like those guys I had seen at MECCA Arena.

Ok, so it wasn't exactly the NBA. But compared to what I had been doing, it was just as spectacular. I was living out a fantasy, staying in hotels, respected by the adult world because of my skills, attracting fans, not cops, selling myself in a positive light instead of selling the crack that could only destroy me.

I thought, "Damn, this is fun. I don't have to worry about looking over my shoulder. I don't have to worry about shooting at somebody or somebody shooting at me. I'm with white and black kids, everybody is acting nice, showing love and high-fiving, a lot of camaraderie. This shit is alright. I can do this. It's easy. Now I've just got to go to school a little more to remain eligible."

Even though I was on the Running Rebels, I still enjoyed playing at the Bryant Center. That was home. And I still loved the challenge of bringing our team into the north side recreation center on the other side of the tracks, but as we all moved into our teens, and more and more of us were involved with weapons and gangs, it could be dangerous to play there. I'm not talking about flagrant fouls, but rather flagrant violations of the law.

There were times I would come into a gym on the north side and score thirty to forty points on one of their players.

I could tell if the reaction was going to turn violent by the number of menacing-looking characters suddenly showing up and hanging out by the exit door.

My guys would huddle up and someone would say, "We are going out the back door, there will be a car waiting for us and we will be out of here."

It was either that or risk having me or someone else get shot walking home.

I remember Junebug telling me, "If a guy like you, who is in the G.D.s, goes on the north side and scores a ton of points on the Vice Lords, you will be a target."

In addition to the Bryant Center, I got involved with the George Bray Neighborhood Center, also on the south side, through Jameel Ghuari, its executive director.

I first met Jameel when I was in the seventh grade at Mitchell Middle School. He was an outreach worker for a gang diversion/drug prevention program. He used to facilitate groups within the middle schools, and I was one of those sent to him by my counselors.

Normally I wasn't very receptive to social workers, but Jameel had a basketball background that fascinated me. He was once under contract to the Buffalo Braves, the team that later moved west and became the Clippers. Jameel also played hoops in Europe, Japan, and the Philippines. Before that, as a young player in Racine, he was best friends with Jim Chones, who went on to play for five teams in the NBA and ABA including the Showtime Lakers and the Cavaliers. That made Chones the most famous player to come out of Racine to that point. Jameel also once roomed at the University of Wisconsin–Parkside with Abdul Jeelani, who had previously attended Washington Park High in Racine and went on to play for Portland and Dallas in the NBA.

Never making it to the NBA himself, Jameel eventually came back to Racine where he has coached AAU basketball and worked with generation after generation of young players, trying to mix lessons on the court with lessons about life.

"I always believed my journey was to get the knowledge, get the experience, and bring it back to this community," Jameel said. "If I would have played in the NBA, I probably wouldn't be doing what I'm doing now. I might be an assistant coach in the league or working as a basketball administrator. I believe the reason I was left here was to help guys like Caron achieve their dreams."

When Jameel first met me, I was thirteen. He said he was impressed both by my size and what he called my "high level of intelligence." But he didn't think I was using that intelligence in a productive manner back then, because he had a pipeline to the street and knew I was selling drugs.

Once asked for his earliest memories of me, Jameel said, "Caron didn't really have a father growing up, so he didn't have any direction. He was like most middle school kids. He didn't really know what it takes to be a responsible young man. At that young age, he was handling a lot of money by selling drugs. The money doesn't make the man. The man makes the money. Caron was not an exception among his peers when you talk about that type of lifestyle."

To try to change some attitudes, Jameel would sit my classmates and me down and describe some of the typical situations we would encounter in the neighborhood. He made it an exercise in role playing.

"You can be the cop," Jameel would tell us, "you can be the drug dealer, you can see the mother who is on crack, taking away resources and focus from her babies and her family, disrespecting her own spirit. Is that what you want for your mom or your sister or your daughter? Of course not, but now you have a visualization of what's real."

For me, Jameel had a personal message: "It is your spirit that, at the end of the day, is going to decide the value of your contribution to humanity."

Those were just meaningless words to me back then.

"I always tried to utilize basketball as a teaching tool for life," Jameel explained, "tried to use the game to relate to young men. I often told them that it wasn't about how much they could get out of basketball, but how much they could give to others through the game. For a lot of young men, it's the glitter that they pursue, but one day, the air is going to come out of the ball, and when that happens, who are they? That's what I tried to teach them, and I think Caron and some of the others absorbed that."

I was more receptive than many others. But no matter how rough or violent his students became, Jameel had a rule.

"I never give up on kids. Never, never," he said. "Nobody gave up on me. You've got to have a short memory with these guys because they are going to do stuff that make you feel they have disrespected you. You have to look at their level of maturity. Do they really understand what they are doing? They are young men who were pampered growing up because they were very good athletes. A lot of the stuff they were doing was limit testing. They always wanted to see how much they could get away with."

Sometimes the kids tried to expand their limits with their fists. When they didn't like Jameel's rules, they wanted to fight him.

One of those kids was a teammate of mine on Jameel's AAU squad when we were the two best players on the club. He was 5'10" and could bench press almost four hundred pounds.

One day, he and Jameel went head to head over a breakfast receipt. Jameel would give us money for food on the road with the stipulation that we brought back a receipt to show how much we had spent.

My teammate and another player hatched a plan to tear a receipt in two and then bring Jameel both halves as if they had paid for two breakfast meals, thus being entitled to double the money.

Jameel just smiled. How dumb did these kids think he was?

When he told my teammate he was wise to his feeble attempt at cheating, my teammate stared back at Jameel and said, "I didn't do that." My teammate was used to getting his way through intimidation. But that wasn't going to work this time.

"Yes you did do it," Jameel insisted.

The conversation was going on in a hotel room. Jameel was sitting at a small table beside one of the beds while my teammate was pacing back and forth nervously.

He was talking louder and louder, threatening Jameel, then suddenly stopping as if he was going to jump his coach.

"Man, chill out," Jameel warned.

"Why, whatcha going to do?"

Under the table, Jameel had a long key in his right hand and he angled it in my teammate's direction as if it were a knife.

"I'm going to tear your ass up," Jameel said.

That calmed the atmosphere down. My teammate had learned his limits. At least that day.

But there were other days when there was no Jameel to calm him down. He is currently serving a fifteen-year prison sentence for breaking the limits set by society.

He wasn't the only hard case Jameel had to deal with. After he threw one kid out of the Bray Center for violating the rules, that kid came back carrying a brick. Jameel picked up a chair and fought the kid off like a matador avoiding a bull.

"Stuff like that happened all the time," Jameel said.

We all had dreams of a life in basketball, but Jameel was always pushing us to think beyond that.

That was hard for us to do as teens who thought we could play forever.

"If you conceive your path to manhood is money, drugs, girls, material things, and you believe it, you can achieve it," Jameel would say. "But once you achieve it, if you have the proper principles and internalize those principles, you realize the paper that money is printed on and other material possessions are just things. They produce energy, but it's not always good energy. The material gains bring a certain level of responsibility. The best way to be worthy of that loan from God is to make decisions based on principle, not just on your bankroll."

"Once we figure out what life is, then we can figure out what we want it to become for us. Certain things fog what life is really about. It's not about pussy, paper, and promoting yourself. Life is about purpose, prayer, and being pointed in the right direction."

His message has never changed over the years, but now that I have lived the dream and am looking beyond it, his words finally resonate with me.

NINE

MY ARREST: SMOKING GUN, SMOKING STATION WAGON

One afternoon, the bullets were really flying at the 18th Street park.

It started when some gangsters showed up from Chicago. At least I think they were from Chicago. Hard to say for sure because they were all wearing Jason masks, like the character in the *Friday the 13th* movies.

One person got shot in the lower back. Someone else got hit in the hand.

I pulled out my own gun and fired away, then took off, not about to wait around to assess the body count. My friends and I scattered in all directions. Since my house was close, that's where I headed.

I made it there safely and plopped down on the couch, my body sweating profusely, my heart beating furiously.

Finally, it got quiet. I didn't hear any more shots being fired or angry yells being exchanged.

But just when I figured it was safe to relax, I heard loud knocking on my front door.

Rap! Rap! Rap!

There was no way I was opening that door.

I was able to crawl over to the sheet covering the window and peek out. It was the police.

Rap! Rap!

I could hear them moving around to the back of the house.

I thought, "Oh shit, they are really looking for me. Maybe they think I shot one of those boys."

I didn't move. Thirty minutes went by. Forty-five minutes.

Fortunately, my mother and brother weren't home, so I didn't have to worry about either of them being spotted moving around.

Finally, the cops gave up and left, but they didn't go far. Looking out the window, I could see them searching all over the neighborhood.

After a couple of hours, with the cover of darkness approaching, I softly opened the back door, snuck out, and made my way through the back alleys to the park.

When I got there, someone told me, "The police are looking for you, for Black Rob, and for some other cat."

"Sh-i-i-it, I didn't shoot those boys," I said.

That was the truth. I had just been shooting in the air to scatter the crowd.

Innocent or not, I was shaken up. So much so that, when I woke up the next morning, I decided it would be a good idea to do the right thing for a change by going to school. I was attending Case High.

If I had really wanted to do the right thing, I would have left my weapon and my drugs at home. Instead, I tucked my gun into my belt, and put half an ounce of cocaine into a zip-lock bag and shoved it into my jacket pocket.

Even if I had been a model citizen that day, it was probably already too late for me to get back on the right track. The police had been keeping an eye on me for weeks because of a lot of gun, gang, and drug stuff going on in the neighborhood. They were always watching the house. The tension between me and the law was building up.

Sometime that morning, sitting in class, I got a page from a customer. He was looking for coke.

I raised my hand, told the teacher I needed to go to the bathroom, and off I went. When I got in the men's room, my client was there along with a couple of other students who were goofing around. We waited until the room emptied and then we completed the transaction. I pocketed the money, gave him a portion of the drugs, and we headed off in opposite directions.

When I came back to the classroom, I sat down and relaxed. But I barely had time to open my book before there was a knock on the classroom door. The teacher opened it and in came several drug agents, members of ATF (Bureau of Alcohol, Tobacco, Firearms, and Explosives).

This was it, the moment I had long dreaded.

They stood at the head of the class as the lead agent pointed down the row directly at me and said, "Mr. Butler, stay seated and put your hands up. Everybody else in the room, move forward."

The other kids in the class were stunned.

I recognized the faces of some of the ATF guys who I had seen around town working with Racine P.D.

I quickly glanced over at the window. It had thick slats on it, plus we were on the second floor.

"Damn," I thought, "I can't jump from here."

When I slowly started to lower my hands, the ATF guys pulled their guns out.

That got my attention. I put my hands back up, and they surrounded me and put the cuffs on my wrists.

Before the agents had even come to get me, they had found the gun in my locker where I had dropped it off after the transaction. They also discovered the remainder of the drugs on me.

There was no talking my way out of this one.

The agents marched me down to the principal's office where they kept me for what seemed like a long time. A lot of the dudes I had grown up with had heard that the ATF had gotten me and they strolled by to see if it was true.

"What the fuck happened?" one of my friends whispered.

"They caught me," I said, shrugging. "Call my mother. Call Junebug and tell him to get me a lawyer. Call anybody you think might be able to help."

When they were done rounding up evidence, the agents got me up, took me to a waiting squad car outside, and off I went to Racine's downtown jail facility.

My mother wasn't allowed to visit me until the next morning.

I was fifteen.

I didn't have a lawyer, just a public defender. He was horrible. All he wanted to do was to get me to plead guilty, get the whole thing over with as soon as possible because he had other clients waiting.

He didn't value my life.

"Take a two-year plea," the public defender told me. "That's nothing. You'll be out in no time."

"Two years?" I said. "Fuck."

When I came into court for a hearing, I was in handcuffs and also had my ankles shackled.

My grandmother and mother cried when they saw me. That made me feel a lot worse than anything the cops were doing to me. My grandmother was working two jobs, my mom two or three jobs so I would have a better life, so I would never get in situations like this. They never knew about all the things I was doing on the streets. They were the most important people in my life and I was hurting them. Instead of respecting them for how much they had sacrificed, I was following the trail of my Uncle Richard and Uncle Carlos.

I know I had vowed to change in the past and had finally started taking my mom's lectures seriously. But I kept losing my resolve, kept falling back into my old bad habits.

As I sat there in the courtroom, I told myself, "I can't do this shit no more. I gotta change. Gotta change."

As the legal process played out, I made five appearances in court. The prosecutor made sure he got all the time he needed to present my entire criminal record. And believe me, that took some time. Even I was surprised at how much they had on me. Yes, there were the assault and battery charges, carrying a weapon, and attempts to deliver drugs. Nothing new there. It seemed like I had been everywhere I shouldn't have been.

But what blew me away was the number of times my name was mentioned in other cases.

Anytime a guy got arrested for selling drugs on a Racine street corner, the police would ask him where he got the stuff. Hoping to get a lighter sentence, the person in custody would give them the name of the dude who had supplied him with the dope. That dude's name was then put in the police paperwork.

It seemed like I wound up in everyone's paperwork.

"Who'd you get the drugs from?"

"It was him."

"And how about you? Where did your drugs come from?"

"Him."

"And you?"

"Yep, him."

That "him" was me every time.

"With all the shit you got going on," the prosecutor told me, "we are going to put it all together and run the sentences concurrently."

I pleaded guilty to everything. What choice did I have? Once they hit me with everything, I threw my hands up and said, "With all the stuff you have on me, fuck it, just give me whatever sentence you want."

I was brought before a judge named Boobanis, a stern-looking man who examined my previous record, spread out in front of him, and then glared at me as I stood before him.

"You did what?" the judge said as he glanced back at my record. "You were where?"

As he went through each case I had been involved in, I lowered my head because it seemed like he was going on forever.

"Fleeing the scene of a shooting," said the judge, reading out loud. "Reckless endangerment. You are a menace to society."

As he looked up to address me, he saw that my head was down.

"Look at me!" said the judge, his voice getting louder, his face turning red. "Look at me when I talk to you. You think this is a joke?"

I was holding my head down so I didn't cry in front of my mother and the rest of my family and friends.

I took a deep breath and sighed a few times.

There wasn't another sound in the courtroom. Even with my head down, I could feel all eyes boring in on me, especially those of the judge.

Finally, regaining my composure, I said quietly, "I made a bad decision."

"You made a bad decision over and over and over and over again," the judge said.

And then he gave me my sentence: Two years.

That hit me hard because I didn't expect anything that harsh the first time I went in front of a judge. But they had thrown so much at me that I guess a sentence that had been any more lenient would have seemed soft.

Two years might not seem so bad to a hardened criminal, but when you are fifteen, that's one-eighth of your life.

In my eyes, I wasn't guilty of anything really bad. But listening to a reading of all the things I had done, I realized I was living life on the edge. The reality was, what the judge was saying was true.

Still, as scary as that moment was, a part of me, the gangster part, thought it was pretty cool. Remember that in the '80s and '90s, when guys were put behind bars, there was an element of the society I came from that cheered them on. The respect they got when they got out of jail made it seem like they were returning war veterans. They were heroes. The guys in the hood celebrated them. They were honored for the time they spent away.

People would help them to get back on their feet financially. Everywhere they went, people would stuff bills in their pockets, $200, $150, $100, whatever people could afford.

"We salute you for doing your time." That's what those released from incarceration were told.

So, while I certainly didn't want to go to jail, I smiled as I imagined the admiration that would be showered on me by the community upon my return.

At first, I was in a Racine jail cell by myself, then they gave me a couple of cellmates.

After three months, I was told that I was being transferred to the Ethan Allen School, a correctional facility for boys in Wales, Wisconsin, forty-five miles from Racine.

Not long before we departed by police van, I got the attention of Jeff King, a correctional officer I knew pretty well, and told him with great urgency in my voice, "I got to let my mother know when I'm leaving because otherwise, she won't know how to get to Ethan Allen."

There were, of course, no GPS apps in those days. If you wanted directions to your destination, you had to go to a gas station to get a map.

The last time I had seen her, my mom had said, "If you are transferred, I need to trail the van so that I know where you are going."

Thank goodness Jeff was a good guy. He pulled me aside and let me make a quick collect call to my mom before we left.

Many officers wouldn't do that, figuring you were calling for help to pull off an escape, but Jeff knew I was neither that desperate nor that dumb.

When she got on the line, I said, "Mom, I'm about to leave."

"Okay," she told me, "I'll rush over right now. I'll be there in a few minutes."

As the officers finished shackling me and the other prisoners and started loading us into the van, I could see my mother's station wagon in the distance, approaching at a high speed.

Before I ducked into the van, I nodded my head at her. She waved back and honked her horn.

When we pulled out, she was right behind us.

The drive to Ethan Allen took about an hour. Seated in the back of the van, with a view of the road behind us through the narrow, thick windows, I could see the station wagon all the way except for a few brief interruptions when other vehicles came between us.

I later found out that drive had been a constant struggle for my mom because she had to keep wiping away tears to see the road.

"Oh, that's my baby," she kept telling herself. "My baby is going away." I had never been away from home before.

As we got close to Ethan Allen, disaster struck. My mom's old station wagon, pushed to the limit in her frantic effort to stay close behind us, started overheating, smoke coming up from under the hood.

Panic started to grip me. I imagine it gripped her too. Here she was alone all the way out there. Even though I was heading for a long stay in a correctional facility, I was thinking about her more than what awaited me.

Forced to slow down, my mom could see the van disappearing down the road. But then, through the tears and the fears, something else caught her eye. It was a sign by the side of the road that read "ETHAN ALLEN SCHOOL."

It was right there.

She pulled over on the shoulder as it started to get dark, turned off the motor, put her head on the steering wheel, and waited for the steam to subside.

When it finally did, my mom turned the car back on, held her breath as she pushed the gear into drive, and smiled for the first time since the trip had begun when the car moved slowly forward.

She made it into the parking lot at Ethan Allen, where she sat for about an hour, looking at the lights in the buildings and wondering which one I was in and what was happening to me.

Finally, at least satisfied to know the location of the facility where I'd be for the foreseeable future, my mom began her sad trip back to Racine.

When she got home, my Uncle Richard, trying to make her feel better, told her, "Only two things can come out of selling drugs. Either you go to jail or you go to hell. Be glad he went to jail."

TEN

MY TIME IN THE HOLE: JUST ME, MY BIBLE, AND MANDELA

The House of Refuge for Juvenile Delinquents was the first facility for troubled youth in the state of Wisconsin, authorized to operate in Waukesha in 1857. In 1959, with the doors to the Waukesha juvenile center soon to close, some of the inhabitants were transferred to a new facility, the Wisconsin School for Boys, located just north of Wales on the property of the former State Tuberculosis Sanitarium. Next to Lapham Peak State Park, the site encompasses 216 acres, seventy-two of them within the perimeter fence.

The first of ten new housing units, known as cottages, was opened in 1960. Wishing to identify the facility as more of an educational institution, rather than one more closely resembling a penitentiary, and perhaps to make the inmates feel they had the opportunity to be students rather than just inmates, Superintendent Roland Hershman renamed the academic section of the facility the Ethan Allen School, choosing the name of the Revolutionary War hero. In 1976, the entire facility was officially changed to the Ethan Allen School by the state legislature. In 1994, a state-of-the-art maximum security building was constructed.

The Ethan Allen School was closed in 2011 by Wisconsin governor Scott Walker and the state Department of Corrections as part of a program to cut Wisconsin's budget deficit.

I didn't know or care about the history of the facility when I first got there. All I knew was that it was 7:30 at night when we arrived and we were told we would be checked in immediately because we had to be in our cells and accounted for by 9:00.

I was wearing the same clothes I had on when I was arrested three months earlier. While I was downtown in the county jail, I wore a prison suit, but they had allowed me to put my old clothes back on for the trip to Ethan Allen.

For a procedure called "intake," I was first brought into a room so big that it looked like a warehouse. The prison officials began by ordering my fellow inmates and I to strip down in order to undergo the squat routine, which consists of spreading your cheeks, coughing, lifting your feet up, and allowing the examiners to check inside your mouth. It was the same routine I had been through at the jail in Racine even though I had remained in the custody of law enforcement officials since then. Once they took our measurements, they gave us government-issued prison outfits.

They also asked us what shoe size we wore. They only went up to a size 12, tough on me because I wore a 13. We were given white sneakers with two straps made of Velcro.

Those shoes caused my toes to cramp up badly. It has messed up my feet ever since. I have corns on my feet to this day because of those shoes.

They gave me boots as well. Same thing. Size 12. I guess I could have cut the front open to let my feet breathe, but then I would have been hit with damaging government property. They would have probably slapped me with another charge for that.

When I was at Ethan Allen, I would take my shoes off all the time to ease the tightness and pain. After a couple of months, I just got used to having my feet balled up in the shoes. I even played basketball like that.

After the indoctrination process, a couple of other guys and I were put in a van and taken to Lapham Cottage, the transitional housing unit. There were kids there from Chicago and all over Wisconsin from Milwaukee to Madison.

Each of the twelve cottages on the property had a name and a distinct group of prisoners. Everyone in Lapham Cottage was waiting to see a counselor who would find out what their particular issue was and then direct them to the proper cottage. One cottage had all gang members. Another housed inmates suffering from alcohol and drug addictions. There was a cottage for prisoners who were in Ethan Allen for shorter periods like a few months. There was even a gay cottage, so that part of the population would feel comfortable. Johnson Cottage, where I wound up, was for drug dealers. There was no division by race. Where inmates stayed was based solely on their issues.

At the front of Johnson Cottage was a huge day room filled with tables and chairs. The furniture was drilled into the floor so that, if guys got into a fight, they couldn't lift the tables and chairs in order to use them as weapons. Down the hall on the right were two offices, one belonging to the counselors, the other to the parole officers.

There were sixteen cells down each of the two halls. When we newcomers were marched down the block to our cells, all the other prisoners jammed their faces up against their bars to get a better look at the new arrivals to see if they recognized anybody. I didn't recognize any of them.

Blacks made up 90 percent of the Ethan Allen inmate population. There were guys in there all the way up to age twenty-one. At that point, anybody who still had time to serve was transferred to a regular prison where, depending on the severity of his sentence, he might spend the rest of his life. So, as I soon learned, I was in there with some desperate people.

Because I was one of the youngest guys, I felt I had to show from the start that I could take care of myself. So as soon as I was put in my cell and the door banged shut, I dropped to the floor and started doing pushups, trying to create an image of "Don't fuck with me. Don't come around me."

I also did it because I wanted to cool down my emotions and get rid of some of the energy and nervousness that had built up within me.

Everybody was looking at me driving my body up and down on the floor, thinking, "Who *is* this dude?"

When I was done, I plopped down on my bed and started mentally preparing myself for the long marathon ahead.

They told me I could get on a fast-track program named Merit that could earn me a release in four months. I knew, at the worst, I'd be home in two years.

The cell had a toilet, bunk beds, and a TV.

I was up pretty much that whole first night. I was mad more than anything else, thinking, "Why the fuck me?" I was still in denial, feeling sorry for myself.

What little sleep I got came to a jarring end at 6:00 a.m. when a guard clanged open my cell door to announce that it was time for breakfast. I'll never forget that clanging sound. When I heard that noise, it rattled through my body. Every time. To this day, when I hear a clanging sound, it rattles me.

Two days after I arrived, I was given a cellmate. He was in there for twenty years for murder. He would sing to himself at night, the song soon turning into furious outbursts that ended with his nonstop screaming. He was crazy. No question about it.

I knew I could fight him if I had to and hold my own. But it was an uncomfortable environment, especially for a teenager. After a few days of that, I was taken to my first meeting with my caseworker. When she asked how everything was going, I didn't hold back.

"I'm doing my time," I told her, "but my cellmate is a problem. He screams and often wakes up in wild fits. I can't function around that shit. I got time to do, too, and he's driving me crazy."

The caseworker listened and got results. I soon had a new cellmate, a guy from Kenosha, Wisconsin, named Lloyd Randle. He was around my age and also in there on drug charges. I still see Lloyd occasionally to this day because Racine and Kenosha are only ten miles apart. When I hold charity events in Racine, he will come up to support me.

I quickly got on the kitchen crew in Ethan Allen. I liked the duty, but it meant I had to wake up between 4:45 and 5:00 a.m., get to the kitchen, and help make breakfast for seventy to one hundred inmates. We prepared eggs, toast, bacon, potatoes, orange juice, and occasionally some rice with raisins in it. We in the kitchen crew would eat first and then serve everybody else. We changed the menu every few days so people would have some variety in their meals.

We had free time, a little extra on the weekends. I could go to the day room after breakfast for two hours and play cards, watch one of the two big TVs, or I could just go back to my cell to chill out.

A food truck came by in the morning to drop off lunch packages for every cottage. The food was similar to the free lunches we got in public school. It was usually cold food like sandwiches, but sometimes, there were items that could be heated up.

At one in the afternoon, we got another two hours of free time. If the weather was good, not often the case in winter, we could submit a request to pass up the day room and go straight to the basketball courts outside. That was my favorite time.

At 3:00 p.m., it was back to our cells until 6:30. Then, we, the kitchen crew, made dinner for everyone. It would usually be a hot meal consisting of some sort of meat and mashed potatoes.

After dinner, we were all allowed a quick collect call—mine was usually to family—and then lockdown, all too quickly it seemed, at 8:30.

A lot of the food was pretty bad, meals slapped together using whatever leftovers were available. If the other inmates had seen what I saw while working in the kitchen, they would have probably been too disgusted to eat. I don't know how we survived on that stuff, but we made it.

That's why we all looked forward to the day, once every two weeks, when we got a real treat, an opportunity to order from the corner store everyone called the canteen. The place had Oodles of Noodles, cupcakes, sodas, chips, all sorts of junk food. I know that noodles in a cup doesn't sound like much of a delicacy, but when you are stuck eating the same type of food every day, anything different can seem like a real feast.

The catch was, we inmates had to pay for our treats. The night before canteen day, the guards would slip an order form under our cell door. We could spend up to $50. That might sound like a lot, but it didn't seem like quite so much once we saw the prices. A six-pack of soda was $10. Five bags of chips cost $18.

I quickly learned that, if I wanted to enjoy some canteen food, I had to earn it by being on my best behavior. If I broke a rule, I could be fined. Even though, like the other inmates, I got my money wired to me by my family, prison officials, who held the payments from home in individual accounts, had no hesitation about taking some of it to pay off a fine levied for some infraction.

Those inmates who were able to get the full $50 and keep it would fill up their cells with so many goodies from the canteen that they wouldn't have to eat the kitchen meals for several days.

For me, there was nothing better than popping open the door of the day room microwave oven, heating up some Oodles of Noodles in a cup, and just chilling. That's what some people did throughout the duration of their stay. Every day, Oodles of Noodles.

I played basketball every day in Ethan Allen. We had a league in which all twelve cottages played against each other, and we had a prison team that faced other correctional facilities.

Every cottage had its own full basketball court in front with a key painted on the concrete. That was it. We didn't have any refs. We called our own fouls, but in reality, the only thing we called was out-of-bounds. Other than that, there was no such thing as a foul.

We played five-on-five with the winner being the first team to 21 points. We'd play for money when we had it, or soda, chips, and other goodies to take back to our cells. I was good enough to almost always win.

I also played some card games, usually pitty pat (similar to gin rummy) and blackjack, but basketball was my thing. And I had the cash to prove it.

As a result, I always got picked first when we chose up teams and that happened almost from the start of my days at Ethan Allen, but I wasn't the tallest guy on the courts. There were some real bigs. One of the taller guys was someone I knew from Racine named D.J. He was in there on a gun charge. Unfortunately, he committed suicide at Ethan Allen, hanging himself.

While my confidence grew once I got settled in the institution, I never got over being scared because of all the stuff that happened there all the time. Ethan Allen was no country club.

D.J. wasn't the only guy to hang himself. And I saw young men being taken advantage of by older inmates. I saw bloody towels all over the place, evidence of the many fights constantly erupting. I saw guys beaten up really bad. An inmate would go into a shower, someone would distract the guard who was supposed to be watching that area, and three other inmates would then rush in and attack the guy in the shower. I could hear the victim screaming followed by the loud footsteps of guards, the rattling of keys, and the lockdown that would automatically follow.

There were a lot of gangs in Ethan Allen. I linked up with a gang of guys I was familiar with from Racine. The gang conflicts were based on race at first. But once the inmate population became overwhelmingly black, the battles were more of a neighborhood thing. The north side would roll against the south side and vice versa.

The worst violence occurred when inmates from one gang were passing around "scripture"—the term for the written rules of a gang—and a rival gang member stole part of it. The situation turned into chaos after that. There were fights in the day room, outside, everywhere. People were getting stabbed with pencils. The guards took all sharp objects away from us, there were lockdowns all the time, and a steady stream of people were sent to solitary confinement.

At the time, the guards didn't carry weapons. No guns. Not even billy clubs, which probably wouldn't have worked anyway unless a guard was a ninja or Bruce Lee.

When a situation threatened to get out of control, the guards would call for backup. There were four, sometimes five people on duty at a time. When thirty inmates announced in unison, "We don't give a fuck!" it was time to call for the backup.

There were times when the guards had to take cover in a bunker situated in the middle of the day room. They would lock themselves in there and then call for help.

I received my calls from family, but I had a thin visitation list. My mom, grandmother, aunts, and my brother were the only ones who came to see me. My mom was there every week. Visiting periods were in two-hour afternoon segments running from 1:00 to 7:00. Visitors could come any day, but I preferred Saturdays because on that day, they could stay four hours.

We met our visitors in a large room where we could sit down and talk with no barriers. Or we could go outside where tables were set up.

The only stipulation was that we had to abide by the ten-second rule. When we first greeted our visitors, we were allowed ten seconds to hug and kiss, but we then had to separate. And believe me, the guards counted every second. I'm surprised they didn't have a clock with tenths of a second like they do in the NBA.

When my mom came, she always went over to the canteen to buy me food and drinks. Seeing her was kind of shocking because her beautiful hair was cut drastically short. She admitted to me that keeping it long was no longer an option because so many clumps of her hair had fallen out, the result of the stress she was under due to my imprisonment.

"It hurts when your child is locked up," my mom said.

She was also shocked sometimes to see me because, being light-skinned, any bruises I got from fighting showed up bright and ugly. And I got my share of bruises.

My mom often brought my little brother, Melvin Jr., with her even though it was always a highly emotional experience for him. He would cry and cry, asking why I couldn't come home with him.

"He can't. He's got to stay longer," my mom would tell Junior.

Only seven at the time, he didn't understand.

"I'm mad at those guards," Junior would say. "I want to beat them up because they won't let my brother go."

"Honey, they didn't lock him up," my mom would tell him. "It was the other police that brought him here."

After I had finished my three months of the Merit program, I was feeling pretty good. One more month and I'd get an early release and be on my way home.

The program was no big deal. After breakfast, I'd be put in a group where we sang songs and did pushups and jumping jacks. Nothing different than I'd be doing on my own. But all it took was an exchange of words, a couple of shoves, and my world came crashing down, the door to my freedom slamming shut.

A small segment of the Ethan Allen population belonged to a gang called the Latin Kings. One of their members referred to me one day in passing as a Hook. That meant a Vice Lord. I told him I was a Gangster Disciple. He said something, I said something, and then he responded with, "Fuck you and your Racine niggers."

He had lit my fuse. I pushed him and things escalated rapidly.

Next thing I knew, the guards jumped me, threw me in my cell, and the whole cottage was put on lockdown.

Soon I heard the sound of keys bouncing off each other on the belts of the guards. I could tell from the volume of the noise that there were a lot of guards and, as the noise got louder and louder, that they were headed to my cell. They brought bad news. I was being kicked out of the Merit program and would be getting a new cell.

Not just any new cell, but solitary confinement, better known to all of us as The Hole.

Fortunately, they gave me a couple of minutes to pack up my few belongings. I used the time to write down the phone numbers of my mother and grandmother, pass the information to Lloyd, and tell him, "Hey, man, when you are allowed a phone call, please call them collect and just let them know I got into a little incident. Tell them not to worry about me. I'm okay. I'll be out soon."

I was placed in back of a vehicle that looked like a police car but with wire mesh wrapped around the doors and windows.

I was driven to a cottage I hadn't seen before, a place that looked foreboding. We were already in an institution surrounded by a high perimeter fence, but this particular cottage had double barbed wire all around it and extra security with double or triple the number of guards at Johnson Cottage.

There were sixteen cells, each much smaller than the one I had just come from.

While I thought my old cellblock was depressing, it was Club Med compared to this one. This was a much different atmosphere, darker and more menacing. Even the guards seemed tougher.

The cells themselves were bleaker. There were no visitors allowed, no roommates permitted, no TV, no electronics, no day room, no recreation, no play time of any type.

There was also no microwave, no Oodles of Noodles. Just a food tray passed under the bars three times a day.

Other than that, there was nothing. Just a lot of time to find yourself.

I was locked up twenty-three hours a day, only allowed out for the remaining sixty minutes.

The hallway was extremely dark, probably because the sun set on the other side. A lot of the cells around me were empty because everyone in the institution wasn't acting up at the same time. There were only a few of us deserving of this extra punishment in any given period.

My cell was pretty dark with only a narrow window that let in a few rays of natural light from the outside. That was pretty much it for me in terms of illumination. In my old cell, I could see the back hill up to the fence. Now, all I saw was a lot of barbed wire so close it seemed like it was going to swallow me up.

During my one hour out of the cage, I was allowed to take a shower, brush my teeth, wash my face, or walk around in this cottage's day room, a miniature version of the one in Johnson Cottage. I wasn't permitted to go outside at all.

The first two days in The Hole, I just slept. The guards told me about the one-hour break I was allowed, but I wasn't interested. Didn't even want to shower. I just stayed in my cell.

By the third day, however, my thoughts together, I came out to enjoy the cleansing feeling of hot water pouring down on me from a shower nozzle.

At first, time dragged, much more so than it had in the main section of Ethan Allen where there were various activities to stimulate the mind.

I got so bored in The Hole that I focused on learning to tell time by the position of the sun. I knew it was April. When I saw the first shadows creeping into my cell in the afternoon, I figured it was about 4:00 p.m. When the sun's rays reached the end of my bed, I estimated it was about 5:00 or 5:30.

It's amazing how, if you work at it, you can adapt to any situation you are thrown into.

I heard a lot of talking from the other occupied cells, but I didn't interact with anybody. It was easy for me to stay out of everybody else's business because I was in the last cell at the end of the hall.

Just like in the main cellblock, inmates jumped up and pressed their bodies against their cell doors when someone new came in, straining to see the latest offender to earn a trip to The Hole.

That's understandable. Anything that breaks the monotony of the same routine, same faces can be stimulating.

Not for me.

When my grandmother heard from Lloyd what had happened, she sent me a Bible along with a message to pray. That Bible was my stimulation. I stayed in bed, pulled it out from under my pillow, read it for a while, put it back under the pillow, stared at the ceiling for about an hour while praying and letting the new material I had consumed register in my brain, then pulled the Bible back out, read some more, lay there for a little bit, and then went to sleep.

I did that every day. Reading that Bible opened my eyes and made me stronger, helping me a lot during those dark moments when I had nobody to communicate with, no one to reach out to. I had to dig really deep to get through that time. It was really frustrating.

I had been in the downtown jail and in the general population at Ethan Allen, but it took this stay in The Hole to make me feel for the first time the pain of having my freedom and my rights stripped away. I was just a number slotted in to do the time.

When a guard told me what to do or where to go, I could protest, but he would win the argument every time. Actually, it wasn't even an argument. It was an order. Dispute it and all I would get was an extended stay in The Hole.

You see a lot of guys lose their sanity when they go through situations like that. Because they are not prepared to function in such lonely conditions, they act even worse than they had acted to get thrown in there in the first place. I got stronger mentally, enabling me to navigate my way through until my release.

I thought a lot about Nelson Mandela. Don't get me wrong. I'm not for a minute equating what he went to prison for, a patriot opposing apartheid in his country, to what I had done to wind up behind bars. But in thinking about him being locked up for twenty-seven and a half years, it made me respect him even more. I tip my hat to him for mastering the art of patience.

I can't imagine being in prison for twenty-seven and a half years. I know what I'm capable of. I might have been able to do five years at the most before completely losing my mind.

As bad as Mandela's long sentence was, it was made even worse by the horrible treatment he received as a strong activist for equality imprisoned in a racist country. Prison officials disciplined him severely, trying to break him.

Ultimately, thinking about him and reading my Bible inspired me. I broke down crying as the realization struck me that I was far different from Mandela or the people I was reading about. There was nothing noble about my cause.

I vowed to change. Nothing new about that. So many times previously in my life when I got in trouble, I had made that vow, but when the punishment I received seemed like nothing more than a slap on the wrist, I thought, "This ain't so bad." That's even the way it was when I first got to Ethan Allen. As scared as I was standing before that judge, once I figured out how to survive behind bars, I was okay, so why change?

I can honestly say, up until the point when I went into solitary confinement, I was pretty much like everybody else in Ethan Allen, going to jail to be a smarter criminal, a better criminal.

Talking to the other prisoners merely reinforced that attitude. When I explained to them how I had wound up in Ethan Allen, they would tell me how I could avoid getting caught in the future, or the plans they had conceived to outsmart the cops once they got out.

But this time, I was infused with renewed determination to alter my ways. "I'm going to do better no matter what it takes," I told myself. "No matter what obstacles are put in front of me, I'm going to get over them, going to get around them, going to bust through them. I'm going to make it. Failure is not an option . . . Failure is not an option . . . Failure is not an option . . ."

I knew I was going to be stuck in solitary for at least a week because that's the minimum when you get caught in hand-to-hand combat with another inmate. I wound up being in The Hole nearly two weeks. Good thing it wasn't longer because I don't think I could have made it through another week.

Instead, I heard the words I had been waiting for. A guard came by to tell me I was going to get out in twenty-four hours.

Not out of Ethan Allen. Just out of The Hole. That was more than enough for me at that moment. Compared to where I had been, the main section of Ethan Allen was going to be a piece of cake.

I hadn't seen the guy from the Latin Kings who had started the whole thing since we had both gone into The Hole. Prison officials had wisely put us at opposite ends of the cottage to make sure there was no rematch. Once we both got back into the general inmate population, we had a few staredowns, but that was about it.

I had no intention of doing anything that could result in a return to The Hole. Before I even got out of there, I had rehearsed how I would react if I got into a situation similar to the one that put me in there.

I knew guys were going to test me. That's what they did in Ethan Allen.

I decided I'd be the bigger person. I was not going to let the goading, name-calling, and threats, all the bully tactics, faze me. If I had to fight, I would do it with my mouth rather than my fists.

I may not have liked that, but I accepted it as the best option.

I had gone from seeing my release date slide from a month away to eleven months. I was not going to slip back any further.

From then on, I never stuck my nose into other people's conflicts. And if guys got loud and ran their mouth in my direction, I had some slick lines to fire back at them. They respected me as a trash talker and didn't try to push me to the next level.

That's because I had built a reputation as a fighter. People talk. While we were going at it verbally, they would whisper to each other, "Alright, leave him alone because it could escalate. And if it does, he *will* fight. He just came out of The Hole."

Nobody talked about kicking my ass anymore and that was fortunate for them. And when new inmates came in, they were warned about messing with me. I got by on my reputation until I got released. I did what I had to do to get through.

My biggest mistake in Ethan Allen, getting into that fight with the Latin King inmate, turned out to be the best thing I could have done because it kept me out of trouble from then on.

Just before I went into The Hole, I had received some jarring news from my mother. I had a daughter, Camary, born that day in Racine.

The news wasn't unexpected, but it hit me hard, feelings of joy, guilt, shame washing over me, giving me plenty to think about for the rest of my time in Ethan Allen and beyond.

I grew up without a father in my life. Most of the men in my family had kids. They were dads, but they weren't fathers. They couldn't be there for their children because they were in and out of correctional facilities. I wanted to embrace fatherhood. To do so, I knew I had to take life more seriously.

The next time my mother visited me, after I got out of The Hole, she brought me a picture. "This is your daughter," she said.

I had heard that the mother, Danisha Harrington, was pregnant, and after a blood test, it was confirmed that I was the father. My mother used to get condoms for me from Planned Parenthood, but I didn't use one that time.

Danisha and I were childhood friends. We'd known each other almost our whole lives.

Once it was established that Camary was indeed my daughter, law enforcement officials tried to charge me with non-consensual sex. We were both kids. I was fifteen and Danisha was fourteen at the time she got pregnant. I was put in a police transport van and driven back to Racine for a court appearance.

The day they took me, Uncle Carlos was on the front page of the local paper after he was caught in the raid in Aunt Tina's basement where Junebug's drugs were found.

One of the police officers in the front of the van yelled back at me, "Hey Butler, you related to this other Butler guy?"

"What?"

He held up the newspaper. I had to stretch to see it because I was shackled. I looked at the name and said, "Oh shit."

Uncle Carlos and I were both downtown in the courthouse at the same time. My grandmother bounced back and forth between the two courtrooms to see both of us.

As it turned out, no charges were filed against me. Uncle Carlos was not so lucky.

When he went to prison, I was still in Ethan Allen. He wrote me letters, reminding me of the lectures he had given me when we were both on the streets. Despite all his warnings to me, we were now both behind bars.

While my mom was not happy I was having a baby when I myself was so young, she went to the hospital to see the newborn Camary and took care of my daughter when Danisha went to work. Camary spent a lot of time at our house growing up thanks to my mom, who was always there for her when I couldn't be.

I know there are questions now about Bill Cosby's personal life, but back in my Ethan Allen days, his show was my guiding light. I watched it every chance I got because it was a program about a normal black family.

I had watched the original episodes at home, but it was the reruns I saw at Ethan Allen that I really focused in on. I now had a daughter and I wanted to learn how a strong family functioned.

Don't think I didn't adore my own family. I knew we loved each other. But watching *The Cosby Show*, I realized I had never experienced a life in which a father, mother, and kids were all sitting together at a dinner table eating a full meal. The whole idea of a house in a nice neighborhood, a father going to work and coming home, everybody involved in a regular routine that didn't include fear, violence, and the constant threat of death hanging over the household was foreign to me. That was a lifestyle I had only seen on TV.

There were a lot of family shows on television, but it was *The Cosby Show* that really hit home with me because they were folks who looked like me. I could relate when Theo, Cosby's son on the show, wanted a new shirt or wanted to run with the wrong crowd. It matched up with my life except, on *The Cosby Show*, there was always a happy ending.

Other than my time in The Hole, I watched that show every day when I was behind bars. Every day. I'd watch it in the day room and then I'd watch it in my cell before I went to sleep.

I felt reborn when I got out of The Hole. It was crazy. It seemed like I was free even though I was still locked up. I was actually excited to get on with my time at Ethan Allen. And I was looking forward to getting out because I had a new frame of mind as a result of being in The Hole.

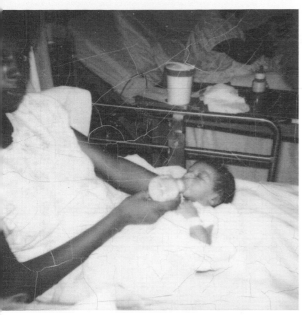

One of the earliest photos of me, a newborn getting a bottle from my mother.

With my grandmother, Margaret Butler Bolton, the matriarch of our family.

My grandmother surrounded by her five daughters. From left to right, Aunt Amy, Aunt Kathy, my mom, Aunt Clarice, and Aunt Tina.

The house I grew up in on Howe Street on the south side of Racine.

Displaying a gang sign at age nine.

With Uncle Carlos on the left.

Horsing around with my friend Li'l Greg at my mom's house in Racine

With Uncle Richard on the right.

Jimmy Carter, aka Junebug, and his wife, my Aunt Kathy.

An illustration of why it was difficult for me, a kid living in poverty, to walk away from the drug trade. This kind of money blinds you to the terrible consequences of being a dealer.

With Detective Rick Geller. His decision to give me a second chance turned my life around.

With Jamie Harris, the man who paid my tuition to get me into Maine Central Institute.

A happy group after my selection by the Heat on Draft Day. From left to right, my brother, Melvin Jr., my mom, me, my agent, Raymond Brothers, my then-fiancée, Andrea, and my AAU coach, Jameel Ghuari.

With Max Good, the coach who put me on the road to UConn and beyond.

In my freshman year at UConn with Coach Jim Calhoun.

As a rookie with the Miami Heat.

With my mom and Jay Leno when I was on his show in 2004.

With Kobe Bryant on the 2004–2005 Los Angeles Lakers during a game against the Houston Rockets. © 2004 GETTY IMAGES. PHOTO BY ANDREW D. BERNSTEIN/GETTY IMAGES

With Coach Pat Riley during a preseason game against the Detroit Pistons in 2002. © 2002 GETTY IMAGES. PHOTO BY VICTOR BALDIZON/GETTY IMAGES

Andrea and I in Cabo San Lucas celebrating our first anniversary.

Andrea and I dancing at our wedding on August 20, 2005.

Posing with a truck used in my "Caron's Coats for Kids" program.

With Gilbert Arenas on the left, a teammate on the Washington Wizards.

Reuniting with Dwayne Wade on January 28, 2009, as a member of the Washington Wizards.
© 2009 GETTY IMAGES. PHOTO BY VICTOR BALDIZON/GETTY IMAGES

As a member of the Oklahoma City Thunder, Kevin Durant celebrates my dunk against the Memphis Grizzlies in Game 7 of the Western Conference quarterfinals during the 2014 NBA playoffs. © 2014 GETTY IMAGES. PHOTO BY RONALD MARTINEZ/GETTY IMAGES

Playing with Caron Jr., when he was three.

With my kids (left to right), Gia, Camaray, Ava, and Caron Jr., with Mia in front in my lap.

When I first went back out on the courts to play basketball, I was like a kid again, being told he could go out for recess.

And for the first time, I thought about taking some of the classes the institution offered. Students could enroll in economics, literacy, math, or African-American history along with computer training. I took some of those classes and became an enthusiastic learner. The whole Ethan Allen routine seemed so easy now.

Each of us had to go before the parole board every ninety days. With my time coming up, I began thinking about how I could appeal to the board for an early release.

I was back on kitchen duty after I got out of The Hole, and it was through that job that I saw my chance, unrealistic as it might have been. I had been informed that, beginning on the following day, I would be part of the crew making the regular food delivery to the staff working in the house that served as the Ethan Allen administration building. That staff included the parole board.

On the night before my first delivery run, I lay in bed and wrote the following letter:

> *Hi, my name is Caron Butler. I went to The Hole and it changed my life. I'm trying to do better. I need to get home to my family. I look at things differently now. If I could do it all again, I would not have done what I did. I have paid my debt to society.*

I understood the risk I was taking. If you write something, nine times out of ten, nobody is going to read it. But if it is read by a staff member or a guard, they might get very angry with you, seeing you as a rebellious inmate. Then you would really have some shit on your hands. How do you fight that?

Nevertheless, I wrapped the letter up and had it in my hand when I went into the office of the head of the parole board to deliver his food.

As I laid out his utensils, I glanced up at him. He did not look like a happy camper. He seemed to be in the middle of some unfolding crisis. I thought, "This is not the day to give it to him."

Instead, I just served him his food, cracked a big smile, gave him a "How are you doing, sir?" and continued on my way.

When I went back into his office a few days later, he appeared to be in a better mood. So I set the letter down quickly on his desk, hoping he wouldn't see it until I was gone so I wouldn't have to face his wrath if he disapproved.

No such luck.

As I started to walk out, he asked, "What's this?"

"That's your meal," I replied.

"No, what's this paper?"

"Uh," I said, hesitating, "it's a letter that I wrote to you."

"I can't read this," he said. "Do you know you can get in trouble for this?"

"I'm so sorry," I told him. "I didn't intend . . ."

"No," he said, interrupting me to repeat his warning even more harshly, "you can get in *trouble* for this."

"I'm so sorry," I said again.

"Take this back."

"Ok," I said.

I grabbed the letter and threw it in the wastebasket right by his desk. Then I rapidly walked out, depressed about his response, hopped on the delivery truck, and took off.

A week later, I went before the members of the parole board. They have the power to release you with the snap of their fingers.

After what had happened with the letter, that was the last thing I was expecting.

I had already been granted one ninety-day defer. That means you must spend at least another ninety days in Ethan Allen followed by another hearing in front of the parole board. I was figuring on a second ninety-day defer.

The man I had left the letter with, the chief parole officer, was at the head of the table. Also at the table were my counselor, my Ethan Allen caseworker, and my caseworker from Racine.

When I sat down, the parole chief asked me, "What did you learn from being in this institution?"

"Learned to be a better person," I said. "Have grown up. Ethan Allen has helped me with structure. Thanks to this institution, I have learned to be accountable."

Before my support crew at the table had a chance to speak for me, the parole chief said, "I believe you. I really believe you. I'm going to grant you a release in thirty days. We are going to start getting your paperwork together.

"And let me warn you, young man, I better not ever see you in here again."

"Yes, sir," I said quietly.

I started to make my way around the table, shaking everybody's hand. When I reached the parole chief, I could see the folder in front of him was open. Sitting in it on top of a stack of papers was my letter, still a bit crumpled from having been wadded up and thrown away by me a week earlier.

I looked down at it, looked up, shook his hand, and our eyes met. He knew I had seen the letter.

He held onto my hand a little longer and then let it go.

Neither one of us spoke.

To this day, I know in my heart that's why I got out of Ethan Allen. I took a chance and it worked out.

When I went back to my unit, I didn't tell anybody what had happened. When they asked, I said, "Those MFs gave me another ninety days. That punk-ass parole board. Ninety fucking days. Can you believe that shit? I've done everything. I'm going to school, I got a job in the kitchen, I haven't gotten into any trouble, no nothing. Yet they keep deferring me."

I did that because, when guys get granted a release, bad things always seem to happen. Inevitably, somebody will do something to try to get the release overturned. If they're not getting out, they don't want anybody else to get out either.

Bursting with excitement, I had to tell somebody. When I got back to my cell, that somebody became Lloyd. I knew I could trust him. "I'm getting out," I whispered. "And soon, bro." He was the only one who knew.

There is a designated group that comes to your cell to handle your official release. On the morning I was getting out, that group came marching down my cellblock.

Other inmates looked up, moved to their respective cell doors, and contorted their bodies to get a good look while yelling, "Who is getting released today?"

The detail opened my cell and I jumped out.

The other inmates were hooting and hollering, saying, "Aw shit, man, why didn't you tell nobody?"

"I will write everybody," I assured them. "I will write you all."

And then, whoosh, I was gone.

My mom and Aunt Tina came to get me. This ride to Wales was a lot more pleasant for my mom than the first time she drove down that road, struggling with her smoking station wagon.

The detail brought me to the area where prisoners are released. Through the glass in front of me, I could see my mom and Aunt Tina.

I wanted to crash through and get the hell out of there, but I still had to go through the checkout process. There was paperwork to sign and my belongings to receive, including the clothes I was wearing when I first arrived. It didn't really take that long, but to me, it seemed like forever.

Finally, I walked through that door, hugged those two women, and it was over.

I had been behind bars for eleven months.

There's an old prison saying, "If you look back, you coming back." I didn't look back.

Never have.

ELEVEN

AFTER MY RELEASE: SHOOTING HOOPS, SHOOTING MYSELF

When I came home from Ethan Allen, everybody in the neighborhood told me how much they missed me. But the only ones who wrote, called, or visited while I did my time were my family, the people who really loved me and cared about me. They were the ones who talked to my caseworkers, and flew up and down that highway in cars that ran hot so I wouldn't be alone on visitors day, investing time and effort to make sure I didn't feel forgotten.

My mother and grandmother had a welcome-home party for me, and it seemed like the whole south side came. But they were just there for the moment. They were coming to see how I looked after being locked up for nearly a year, what I was thinking, whether I was going to go back to my old life.

Those people didn't matter to me. I knew who really worried about my welfare, who wanted me to have a better life, wanted me to avoid making the same bad decisions that had put me on the road to Ethan Allen.

When the party was over and the neighborhood crowd left, my family was still there, telling me how much they believed in me. I wanted to change for them because I wanted them to be proud of me.

I couldn't sleep that first night at home. When I finally got out of bed in the morning, the room was filled with mosquitoes and flies. That's because I had left the windows wide open so I could hear the cars going by. It gave me a comforting feeling, knowing I was back in the city, hearing people driving back and forth, free to go wherever they desired, whenever they felt like it. Those windows stayed open for many nights after I returned.

I'd lie in bed, needing to go to the bathroom, but I'd think, "I'm not going to get up because, at six o'clock, the guards are going to open the cells anyway . . . Wait a minute, I'm not locked up anymore."

The first thing I did on my first day home was to go see my daughter, Camary, who was a couple of months old by that time.

In those first few days, I walked all over Racine, from the south side to midtown and back to the south side because that enhanced my feeling of freedom. It was great to know I could walk out of my house and head in any direction I chose without someone telling me I couldn't go this way or that way.

I appreciated the smallest things after incarceration.

No one I knew could understand the horror of losing your freedom more than Uncle Carlos, who remained in prison for years after I was released. He may have been bitter, but not toward me. He wrote me a lot after I got out and periodically called, telling me to keep my head up and stay straight because, he said, "if you wind up back in prison, you'll have to deal with me."

My mom did her part as well, moving my brother and me into a house in midtown so I could get away from the bad environment on the south side. It was tough to stay straight in the old neighborhood, because the crowd I had run with expected me to be the old Caron. When I told my mom about the pressure I was under, pressure that was even greater than what I had experienced in Ethan Allen, she realized it was time to get out.

Even so, it wasn't like we moved to another town. All of Racine is only seven miles long. So even though I spent most of my time in midtown, my old buddies came around, trying to get me to fall back into my former lifestyle.

Under the terms of my release, I had to wear an electronic ankle bracelet for sixty days. I used it as a crutch to help me walk away from trouble. When guys would ask me to hit the streets with them, I'd say,

"Oh, man, I can't. The parole officer has got me on this bracelet. I can't get more than a hundred feet off the porch. I've been handed some strict rules to follow, but I'll do what I have to do to avoid another stretch in an Ethan Allen cell."

It wasn't entirely true, but it worked.

So what was I going to do with myself? I got a job, a real job, working at Burger King. Now that I had a daughter, it was time to live a life that could make her proud of me someday. I just walked in there and asked if they were hiring. They were. I got the job. If they had known I had been in Ethan Allen, I might not have been hired, but because I was a juvenile, I didn't have to reveal my past.

Nevertheless, it didn't stay secret for long. Soon after I started working there, my pant leg inched up one day, uncovering my electronic bracelet. But by then, I was doing well on the job, everybody seemed to like me, and to the credit of the management, they stuck with me.

Even more important than the chance to earn a little money, working there ate up my free time so I didn't have a chance to go roaming down the streets. Nothing can get you in trouble quicker than boredom. Your friends are the people you grow up with, so it's easy to gravitate back toward them, especially if you've got nothing else to do.

The first paycheck I got from Burger King was nothing compared to what I had been making dealing drugs. It was like $6.50 to $7 an hour, working from 8:00 a.m. to 4:00 p.m. every day while I was also trying to get back into school. After taxes, it came out to about $200 a week, half the amount I used to make in one day selling drugs when I was eleven.

But I would tell myself, "You're staying out of trouble, man." I was finally making an honest buck, no longer poisoning anybody with bad drugs or having to look over my shoulder all the time. I slept amazingly well at night.

My friends didn't give up. When I was working, they would come into Burger King and laugh at me. They'd goad me, saying, "Come on, let's get out of here. Why are you working at a restaurant when you can make so much more hustling dope with us out on the streets?"

Try as they did, they couldn't tempt me. I had spent enough time in the streets to know what comes out of that life. That shit don't change, the laws haven't changed, the game hasn't changed. If you do this, you get that. The young kids think the results will be different because no one before has done it quite like them. Do your homework. Study history. No matter what, it's the same results. You may get away with it a few times, but sooner or later, they're gonna get you.

The peace and quiet of my new life would often be shattered by the random appearance of parole officers. The first three weeks were the toughest, because they would pop up everywhere. Whether I was at work or on the porch, they would swoop in, brakes screeching, and jump out.

"Put your hands up," they would yell. Then they would search me. I didn't get any credit for getting a job. The parole board didn't care.

But after that first few weeks, after they saw I was clean, they were cooler.

My family noticed a difference in me. Uncle Richard told me he could see my head was finally on straight because I wasn't talking about street stuff. My focus was on working, getting back into school, getting back into basketball, and taking care of my new daughter.

"That's when I knew you finally got it," Uncle Richard told me.

I also received some much appreciated support from a cousin, Jarvis McMillian, who told me, "I see a little different drive in you. A lot of people get out of incarceration and say they are going to change their life, go on a different path. But after a couple of months, that gets old and they go back to the same old thing. Not you. You've got a look of determination in your eyes."

I have to admit, though, that my connection to the old days wasn't completely severed. I had stashed away some of the money I had made from drug dealing before I went to Ethan Allen. So in addition to the Burger King salary, I had a cash reserve. And I had no problem with using it. I gave a cousin some money when he needed it. I gave my guy, Li'l Greg, some cash. And I pulled out some for myself when I ran short.

Once I had a job, I concentrated on getting back into school.

I had been arrested at Case High School, part of the Racine Unified School District. Because I had been in possession of both coke and a gun on school property, district officials weren't about to let me back into their educational system.

I appealed to the school board and brought a strong supporting cast with me: my mom, other family members, community leaders, and members of the NAACP. They all spoke on my behalf.

It was wasted breath. The Racine Unified board wouldn't budge. I was out and I was going to stay out.

The board did give me one option. On my way out the door, I was handed stacks of papers in folders. One was on the subject of math, another English, the third sociology.

"What am I supposed to do with this?" I asked.

"Work on this material every day," I was told. "And maybe, by the end of the year, you can pass an equivalency test."

"I don't have a teacher," I said.

"You're going to have to hire a tutor," an official suggested.

A tutor? Really? Between my salary and what my mother was making, we barely had enough to keep food on the table and a roof over our heads. And that cash reserve was dwindling rapidly.

My mom feared we'd have to move to Milwaukee to get me in school, but she didn't want to leave her family in Racine. There had to be a better way.

"Maybe you can go to Gateway," my mother suggested.

Gateway Technical is a community college, but it also has classes for those seeking a high school diploma. There was, however, a big problem as far as I was concerned. Gateway was also part of Racine Unified.

"They aren't going to let me in there," I told my mother.

"Alright," she said, "we are going to use your legal first name. Instead of Caron, you are going to apply as James."

Her father's name was John James. He called her in the hospital after I was born and said, "Will you please name my grandson after me."

My mother told him, "Dad, I don't like that name. I don't want to name my baby after you. I love you, but I don't want to be calling my baby James."

"Please."

So she did.

But my mom told my grandfather, "I'm going to give him the first name James, but I am never in my life going to call him that. I'm doing it for you."

But now, the name she had initially rejected saved us both, allowing her to stay in Racine and me to stay in school.

I enrolled at Gateway as James Butler, got in without so much as a raised eyebrow, attended classes for a semester, then came back to the Racine school board for a hearing and asked to be readmitted to high school.

A lady on the board sternly asked, "How do we know if you could even function in school? You've been out for a long time."

"No," I said, "actually, I've been in school. I've been going to Gateway. And I've been getting good grades. I've got a B average."

Another member of the board looked puzzled. "Your name isn't on the list," she said, her eyes roaming down a sheet of paper in front of her.

"That's because he enrolled as James Butler," my mom responded, standing up in the audience, "and, like he said, he got a B average. He can do this."

My Auntie Tina, sitting in the audience with her emotions bubbling over, cried out, "You can't give up on the kid. Isn't education what the school system is supposed to be all about?"

The board members looked at each other and someone called for a recess.

When we were invited back in, the head of the board asked me to stand—I felt like I was back in court—and said, "Okay, we are going to let you go to school, but under certain conditions. You are going to be under a close watch. (That was automatic since I was still wearing the electronic ankle bracelet.) We heard about you. You have a reputation. We are going to search you whenever we feel like it. And we don't want to hear anything back from you. If you have any problems, you are going to be expelled for life."

So, with something less than a high five and a big hug, the board allowed me to enter Washington Park High School.

It was just as the board member had described. I was on a very short leash. Sometimes they would pull me out of class and pat me down in the hallway in front of everybody. That was something I had to deal with.

But at least I was back in school.

And once they saw me on the basketball court, the fears turned to cheers.

Ultimately, my future depended on basketball. Jameel Ghuari understood that before I did. "Caron," he said to me after my release from Ethan Allen, "why don't you come over and play with our AAU team and get some exposure? It could be the start of a new life for you."

I hesitated at first because Jameel operated out of the Bray Center, located in midtown. Even though I lived there now, I still saw Bray as a rival community center. I was trying to change my life, but my loyalties were still tied to the old gang.

But Jameel's team was in an organized league, a structure we had not had on the south side, and he had the best connections in the area in terms of getting me on the radar of people who could get the word out about my hoop skills.

I talked to some of my south side guys and they encouraged me to play for Jameel. So I agreed to suit up for him.

It was a good team. Five of the top six kids on that squad wound up playing Division I basketball including Brian Bedford and Sharif Chambliss, both of whom ended up on college teams that reached the Elite Eight of the NCAA tournament.

With all the guys coming in and out of my house, there were still drugs around. As I was soon to find out, if the wrong people found them, my future would be lost.

But it was Jameel who first stumbled upon the coke. He had come over to talk to me and found some dope sitting on a dresser in my bedroom.

"Man, come on," he said. "What are you doing? We are trying to accomplish something for our team and for you."

Jameel shook his head, then looked me in the eye and said, "Let's take a ride."

He drove me out to Caledonia, a community northwest of Racine where I currently live with my family. Back then, he took me out there to see the mansions of the Johnson family, owners of Johnson Wax, one of the largest employers in the area.

Proving to be a true visionary, Jameel told me, "Caron, you could live out here someday. But if you want to do that, there are certain sacrifices that you've got to make. Do so and anything is possible. You have the talent. But the greatest power you have is the power to choose. The question is, do you have the willingness to drop some of the things that might hold you back? Will you make that choice?"

I didn't answer him. I knew I had made some big changes in my life, but I also knew I was a work in progress.

Jameel let me stay on the team, but we often clashed. Back then, I know I was difficult to coach. There were times when I didn't want to practice and games I didn't want to play. Because I still had issues accepting authority, it was inevitable we would bang heads.

One of our worst confrontations occurred at a major AAU tournament held in New York in the Bronx.

Jameel had given me a Magic Johnson tape to watch. I played it over and over until I could copy every move Magic made. I would come down the court, turn sideways, shield the ball, assess the defense, and anticipate the offensive flow.

But, according to Jameel, I was too focused on style and not enough on results.

"Caron," he yelled at me during a timeout, "you're not doing anything other than standing there, admiring yourself. You've either got to pass the ball or attack the defense. You're not an entertainer. I need you to entertain by playing your game. We are not going to win by styling. We are going to win by you being in a predatory state, not a performing state. None of this, 'Look at me.' No, show them what you've got."

When I protested, Jameel just waved me away and stormed off.

Yes, I was testing his limits, getting in his face, fighting to impose my will on the team. That type of power struggle may have worked in other facets of my life, but this was a battle I wasn't in a position to win.

"Look, you are not the big pimp on this team," he said after I defied him during a game one time too many. "I'm the big pimp. I don't care about winning or losing. I care about playing this game the right way. So if you don't do what I tell you to do, I'm going to put you on a plane back to Racine. Just try me."

It didn't end there. After the game, Jameel drove the team van back to our hotel in New Jersey, just across the George Washington Bridge, pulled into the parking lot, threw the vehicle into park, jumped out, went around to my side, banged the sliding door open, and said, "Get your ass out. If you don't want to listen, then you won't be here."

Jameel had been around long enough to know that coaches at the amateur level who want to win at all costs, even if it means giving up their principles and the life lessons they want to teach, will ultimately lose. Players will take advantage if they know the coach will put up with anything to get a victory.

"I'm in New York," Jameel told me as we stood in the parking lot. "I'm going to have a good time, win, lose, or draw. I'm going to enjoy my trip. If you want to enjoy it, then you need to play and not fight me mentally and emotionally."

He sprinkled his comments with quite a few four-letter words. Jameel got his point across. I played it his way from then on, and I was a better player for it.

Although I felt good about my new life, I got a jarring reminder that the old days of violence and murder were never far away.

I was on the porch of my house getting my head shaved bald one lazy afternoon when my friend Dre came by.

"Come on, man," he said. "Let's hit the block."

"I ain't fucking around no more," I told him. "I can't do it. I'm going to chill. I'm playing basketball, I'm working, and I got some money. I got some good shit going for me. So I'm cool."

"I'm about to go down to 12th and Highland," Dre said.

That was about five blocks up a hill and around a corner.

He gave me the folks handshake and walked away. I can still see him disappearing in the distance. It's the last image I would ever have of him.

About two hours later, I heard that a guy had shot Dre, and he had been rushed to the hospital.

By the time we got there, people were screaming, "He dead! He dead!"

Shot twice in the chest, Dre never had a chance. He was gone at seventeen.

Memories of the final day of James Barker Jr. exploded in my head. Now I had lost a second friend.

Soon after, a bullet found its way into my body.

The shooter was someone I knew very well. It was me.

I had gone to a dance party at Park High, not dreaming it would end with one of the scariest situations of my life.

Entering the gym, which had been turned into a dance hall, I had my gun tucked into my waistband. I didn't dance, but I didn't want to take my swag away, so I was boogying.

And POW, somehow, some way, the gun went off and wounded me in my left knee. Fortunately, the bullet, after blasting away some skin, wound up buried in the floor rather than in my knee.

That gun had a safety catch on it, but it was off because I didn't know how to work it.

No need to call the police because they were already in the gym, standard operating procedure in Racine when there was a high school party.

Also in the gym were members of other gangs like the 12th Street Highlanders, a group that shared feelings of animosity with my old gang on the south side.

When my gun went off, one of their guys pulled his gun out awkwardly and shot himself in the chest.

We had been fellow inmates in Ethan Allen. When I had first walked into the party, I had nodded at him and said, "What up, man?"

We were cool with each other in Ethan Allen, but back on the streets, he was reunited with his gang and my loyalties were with mine. Didn't matter that I was living in midtown. I was still identified with the south side in the gang mentality.

What happened to the other guy and me that night is evidence of how fucked up we all were. It was just a dance. We didn't need to have our guns in there.

While my wound wasn't life threatening, his was. He almost died. He was rushed to the hospital in critical condition and put in intensive care, life-saving tubes inserted into his body. He survived, but had breathing problems for a long time afterward.

I was scared because I was leaking blood all over the hardwood.

When everybody in the gym hit the ground after hearing the two shots, I took my gun and slid it across the floor.

Then, I got up and limped away. The police started checking everybody as they walked out, but I had already made my escape, accompanied by Li'l Greg, Black Rob, and another friend, Andre Love.

When they saw blood splattered down my pant leg, they were naturally concerned, but I told them, "I'm good. Right now my concern is that I've got a bracelet on and if I don't get home by eight o'clock, forty-five minutes from now, I'm in deep shit with my parole officer."

That was the time my curfew started, although sometimes, the officer would allow me a few extra minutes to walk in the door.

I made it home that night by 8:00. Good thing, too, because if the parole officer had seen my wound, breaking curfew would have been the least of my problems.

As I walked into my bedroom, the wound was bubbling and swelling up, looking like a real bad burn. In addition, the bleeding hadn't stopped.

I knew I should go to the hospital, but with the electronic bracelet on my ankle, if my parole officer was monitoring the signal, he would know that's where I had gone. And if doctors there told him that it appeared I had a self-inflicted wound, I'm sure the parole board would have ruled that I had violated my probation and I would soon be on my way back to Ethan Allen.

Nope, I was going to have to handle this myself. I put a needle in alcohol and popped the expanding bubble of blood. Then, I treated the area with Neosporin.

It took time for that wound to heal, but I was able to function while avoiding limping, so the incident remained a secret to all but my close friends.

I never told my mom what had happened. When she reads about it in this book, it'll be news to her.

The more reminders I had of my old life, from Dre's death to the near-death experience of the rival gang member at the dance to my wounded knee, the more I realized that I needed a ticket to a better world and basketball could be that ticket.

It was the fall of 1997, and at the age of seventeen, I was heading into my first full year of high school, having missed most of the previous two years because of my arrest and imprisonment. I was finally going to get a chance to play a full season of basketball. I vowed to totally focus on my game and see just how good I could be.

Many of the kids I played with and against in high school had a trainer. I couldn't afford one. Nor did I have a vigorous workout routine like they did. But I had my talent and I had a strong will.

"Fuck it," I told myself. "I don't want to be back in the streets. I know what that's like so I'm going to bust my ass and play with a tougher edge than everybody else. And I'm going to make it."

Junebug was there to support me. "You've been thrown right back out there among the wolves," he said, "but basketball can save you."

I remember Jim Betker, who was my P.E. coach at Park High, coached my brother in basketball, and is now Park's head basketball coach, telling me, "If you stay humble and do what you are supposed to, there's a chance for you to make some money playing basketball. Because when you are 6'7", can handle the rock like you do and make shots for yourself or a teammate, the NBA could be in your future."

It was the first time any high school coach had told me that my dreams were not unrealistic. That just fired me up even more.

With so much to shoot for, I finally put it all together on the court in my one full season at Park High, averaging 24.3 points, 11.1 rebounds, 4.3 assists, 2.1 steals, and shooting 55 percent from the floor. I played at such a high level that, at season's end, I was named Player of the County, Player of the Year, and first-team All-State.

Nothing could stop me now. Or so I thought.

Little did I know I was about to be blindsided by a frightening incident that would put me at the crossroads of my life, one path leading to glory, fame, fortune, and happiness, the other to darkness, despair, and ruin.

TWELVE

MY SECOND CHANCE: THE CROSSROADS OF MY LIFE

I was restless and uncomfortable as I lay in bed on a cold January morning in 1998. I tossed and turned, trying to find a position that would allow me to fall back to sleep.

It seemed impossible because of the cumbersome cast, placed on my right hand to help heal a fracture I had suffered on the court playing for Park High.

Adding to my discomfort was a flu bug that had drained my energy.

At least it was quiet in my Bluff Street house in midtown. My mother had already left for work and Junior was on his way to school. Occasionally, from my second-floor bedroom, I could hear the laughter of kids on their way to Park High, located just around the corner.

I wasn't planning on going anywhere, instead taking the day off to shake off the flu. The cast, weighing heavily on me, was a different matter. It would be three more weeks before I could get it removed, leaving my breakout season at Park on hold.

All of a sudden there was the sound of sirens coming down the street. That didn't alarm me. Sirens in Racine in those days were as common as birds chirping. I barely noticed them unless I was doing something wrong.

With the way my life was going then, on the court, in the classroom, and with the job at Burger King, doing something wrong was the last thing on my mind.

So I was puzzled when I heard the sirens stop at the house and the murmur of a crowd gathering outside. I leaned over, peeked my head through the blinds, and saw heavily armed figures in black emerging from a circle of squad cars, flashing lights everywhere.

I still wasn't worried. Like I said, I was no longer the kind of person they'd be interested in.

But it was nerve-racking to hear the sound of pounding footsteps heading up to my porch followed by ferocious banging on my front door. I didn't have the energy to get up, so I just dropped my head back onto my pillow.

There was silence for an instant, then the sound of wood splintering as the invaders broke down the door.

In they came and then up the stairs, a full SWAT team, masks on their faces and who-knows-what on their minds. As I soon learned, the group included my old nemesis, Sergeant Dave Boldus.

Before I had a chance to say anything, one of the cops cracked me on my head with the butt of his gun. I hopped up and lifted my arms toward the ceiling.

The cops led me down the stairs and planted me on the couch. One of the officers pulled out handcuffs, started to put them on me, then stopped, a confused look on his face. He wasn't sure how to deal with the cast. He wound up putting one cuff on my free arm and hooked the other one up to a chair. Helpless, I watched as the cops proceeded to tear up the house.

It was obvious they were looking for drugs.

Again, I wasn't worried. I wasn't in that business anymore.

"There is no dope in this house," I said to anyone who would listen. "And I don't have any guns in this house, either."

The search verified my statements. "Nothing in the house," one of the cops said.

"Go check the garage," ordered the leader of the force.

I could hear them outside, giving the garage the same thorough treatment they had given the house.

But this time, the cops found what they were looking for—a load of crack.

I heard a law enforcement guy yelling, "Bingo! We got it."

It wasn't mine. But it wasn't a surprise to me, either.

There were always people going in and out of that garage from the street, hiding stuff. I understood that. That was the code of the street. You never denied your friends and neighbors access to a safe haven. All I knew for sure was that the drugs did not belong to me.

The cops marched back into the house triumphantly and surrounded me.

About that time, my mother was arriving from work, frantic when she saw the cars with the flashing lights around our house in a semicircle. She ran up to what was left of the front door, but was told, "You can't come in the house, ma'am."

Insisting that she lived there didn't get her anywhere. My mom craned her head to look in and saw me sitting on the couch, shaking my head.

The police huddled and then Detective Rick Geller came over to me and, pointing to the cocaine, asked, "Is this your stuff?"

"No, it's not mine," I insisted.

"The word is there is dope being sold out of this house," Rick said. "There was a drug sale out of this residence earlier today."

Fortunately, an informant's description of the dealer didn't match my appearance.

"Whose drugs are these?" Rick asked. "Not mine," I said once again, my mantra for any cop who questioned me. "I don't get down like that no more. I work. I go to high school. I'm not involved in dope. I don't want to mess with dope. I don't want to have anything to do with dope. I'm trying to get my life back in order."

"Why aren't you in school right now?" Rick asked.

"I wasn't feeling well today," I said. "I've got the flu and I've got this broken hand that's causing me a lot of pain. That's why I was laying down."

"Did your mom call the school to tell them you weren't coming in?" he asked.

"Yes she did. Check the records."

Rick turned and went back into the huddle.

By that point, the police had allowed my mom to come in. When she saw me, her eyes zeroed in on the handcuffs.

"What's going on?" she said

"It's a drug bust, ma'am," she was told.

At first, like me, my mom wasn't worried. Even though she felt confident I was no longer in the drug business, she was always searching the house for dope, to assure herself that I was indeed clean and to make sure nobody else, like Uncle Richard, who had a house key, or Junebug, had brought in any illegal substances. My mom's search became part of her routine whenever she cleaned the house, which was quite often. She would look in my bedroom, my closet, and in the basement. She even searched her own bedroom.

Her concern was understandable because one time, she had actually found drugs. They were in the basement where she had ten boxes of old clothes and other household stuff stacked up.

One day, while trying to pull one of the boxes down, my mom spotted a zip-lock sandwich bag behind the stack. Inside was something that looked to her like a big rock, although, as my mom later told me, "It wasn't shaped like a rock. It looked more like a chunk of cheese."

Cream-colored cheese.

And then, it hit her. It was crack cocaine.

Scared, my mom didn't dare tell anybody.

She had thought about taking the coke over to the police station, but decided that wouldn't end well. "I wasn't going to give them anything to talk about," my mom later told me. "They probably would have started watching our house. I decided it was between me and God."

So, she simply took the dope outside and threw it in the trash can, $17,000 worth of crack laying at the bottom of the garbage.

Maybe some trashman got rich that day.

When I came home, my mom told me she had found crack cocaine in the basement.

"For real?" I said.

Her regular search routine, however, never extended to the garage.

At least there were no weapons in the house the day the SWAT team came barreling in. That would have allowed those cops to hit me with a double whammy just like the day at Case High when the combination of coke and a gun landed me in Ethan Allen.

I later found out there had previously been a gun in our house, a sawed-off shotgun that my great-grandmother had once owned back in Mississippi. She had given it to my grandmother, who had later passed it down to my mom for her protection, always necessary in our neighborhood. But my mom, afraid it would fall into the wrong hands, had given the gun to her great uncle.

When my mom was told by the cops that morning that drugs had been found in the garage, panic started to creep into her mind.

To counter her fears, she quickly and aggressively defended me.

"What drugs did you find?" she demanded to know from Rick. "Get the fingerprints. I know the drugs are not his. He doesn't sell drugs. He doesn't have any drugs."

The cops took my mom out to the garage, the scene of the crime. They had found a piece of a drainpipe laying against a wall. It appeared someone had thrown it there in haste. Inside the pipe were 15.3 grams of crack cocaine, worth $1,500 to $2,000 in street value.

Back in the house, my mom continued to plead my case. She told Rick and the other officers that, after getting out of Ethan Allen, I had promised her that I wasn't ever going back to my old life, that I loved my friends but that it was time to cut the cord and get away from them. She said she believed me, and they should as well.

She also told them that there was easy access to the garage from the street, that sometimes, lying in bed at night, she could hear the garage door going up and people in there. She said she was afraid to confront them. Instead, she had asked the landlord to change the locks on that garage, but he had never done so.

Rick and the others listened, but I didn't think she was making a lot of points with them.

As I sat there, also listening, I got really worried for the first time. The face of Uncle Carlos flashed before me. Was family history about to repeat itself? I thought about him getting caught in Aunt Tina's basement with Junebug and Junebug's crack. I thought about Uncle Carlos's basketball talent and how it was all wasted when he was convicted and sent off to prison, his dreams of college and the good life shattered.

Now I was sitting in the same spot, this Detective Geller about to send me off to the same fate.

All my hard work to reform and go straight was about to go down the drain because of that drainpipe.

If I had known Rick's background as I sat there in despair, I would have been even more pessimistic about my future.

He was a man on a mission.

Rick was a member of the street crimes unit of the Racine Police Department, the equivalent of a drug unit. Now retired, he served in that unit for fourteen and a half years, twenty-nine years in all in law enforcement.

His resolve to go to war with the drug trade was hardened by an assignment that took him to Chicago, where he had worked with a Drug Enforcement Administration agent named Erin Desmond. The pair were hidden in a van on a street in a crime-ridden area, searching for a suspect named in a federal warrant.

As the two sat there, they saw ten drug dealers on that one block, all battling for position as they tried to flag down passing motorists to sell them crack.

Desmond turned to Rick and said, "There are portions of Chicago like this one that we have lost forever."

Thought Rick, "I never want Racine to get to that point."

He worked hard to clean up our town, unwavering in the face of danger. He's so soft-spoken that, the first time I met him, he didn't come across as a tough guy, but I have since heard stories about him that convinced me he could handle himself on the streets.

One night on patrol alone in the area of the 18th Street park, Rick confronted a guy named John concerning a domestic abuse complaint.

John towered over Rick, had twenty-inch biceps, and loved to fight.

"John, you hit your wife so I've got to arrest you," Rick told him.

John looked down at Rick, smiled, and said, "Officer, I don't think you are going to be able to do that."

"You know what, John," Rick told him without blinking, "I agree. I don't think I can take you, but I'll tell you what's going to happen. I'm going to scream into my car radio and twenty of my closest friends are going to show up. I'm still probably going to go to the hospital and you're going to go to the hospital. I really don't feel like going to the hospital. What about you, John?"

John thought about it, then turned his back to Rick, put his hands behind him, and let Rick handcuff him. John was so big that Rick had to use two sets of cuffs to secure him.

Rick's backup officer came racing down the street, jumped out of his car, saw the big guy standing peacefully in handcuffs, and whispered in amazement to Rick, "How in the fuck did you do that?"

It was also not wise to underestimate Rick. He had been after one drug dealer for a long time, but was unable to get the evidence necessary to nail his elusive target.

Confronting Rick, the dealer, a smirk on his face, told the detective, "You're good, but you're not that good. You are not going to get me."

Rick shrugged his shoulders and redoubled his efforts. He enlisted the aid of a high-powered government agency that had high-tech surveillance equipment and eventually got the evidence he needed for an arrest. Rick confiscated nine of the dealer's vehicles, and the guy wound up spending fifteen years in prison.

When Rick and the dealer again came face to face, the dealer told the detective, "I was wrong. You were that good."

In discussing his career, Rick once told me, "It wasn't anything personal. I had a job to do, and the drug dealers had a job they did. Sometimes they won, sometimes I won."

Rick was thorough and relentless. He and the rest of his unit would zero in on homes that were the centers of suspicious activity. In some cases, they found that someone associated with the residence had prior charges filed against him for drug dealing or other crimes. Or there were numerous complaints from neighbors about the type of people congregating around the home or the frequent loud noise level. A lot of visitors coming and going at all hours of the day or night but never staying long sent up a red flag. Obviously, Rick could tell the dope fiends from parents dropping off kids for day care.

To raid a house, Rick needed a search warrant. To get one, he needed informants who could provide evidence that there was drug activity going on inside. He would send them in to make a drug purchase and then bring him the dope. The informants would pay the drug dealer with marked bills.

Rick gave the informants an initial payment of $20 to $40. If the investigation resulted in felony arrests, Rick then gave them an additional $100 per arrest. So a houseful of dealers could result in a $500 to $600 payday for an informant. Rick had no trouble recruiting informants. Some were guys who simply did it for the money, while others were people who were willing to cooperate with police in order to get pending charges against them dropped.

The informants' biggest fear was that their identity would become known around the neighborhood. Then they would have another warrant to worry about, a death warrant from gang members. But Rick had a great reputation among informants when it came to protecting them. There were situations where a defense attorney representing a dealer wanted an informant to testify in court. Rick refused to allow that, willing to drop the charges before he'd endanger his informant.

"I'd lose a case before I'd lose somebody who was working for me," he said.

My house was one of the homes assigned to Rick. When he started his investigation, he had no idea who lived there. He learned that one of the residents was a James C. Butler, the name I was using at Park High. We had never met at that point. Rick also saw some names that he knew were, or had been, involved in drug activity like Richard Butler, my uncle.

Rick sent in an informant who was able to buy drugs at our house. That gave Rick the final piece of evidence he needed to get a search warrant from a judge.

That was nothing new for Rick. During his time on the drug unit, he also spent ten and a half years on the SWAT team. Over that period, he drafted approximately one thousand search warrants, and personally helped execute about four hundred to five hundred of them.

Because his investigation had also turned up my arrest at Case High for possession of a gun, along with cocaine, it was decided to use the SWAT unit for the operation because, as Rick put it, "a name associated with the residence had a weapon in his past." Because of the criminal history of several people associated with my house, the warrant had a no-knock provision that gave the SWAT team, usually consisting of seven to nine people, the right to barge in.

The preferred time to pull off a drug bust was early in the morning, because drug dealers usually operate well into the night and then fall exhausted into a deep sleep after the sun comes up. That made it far less likely that, when confronted by the SWAT team, they would be able to dispose of the drugs or grab a weapon to fight back.

If street-level dealers get caught with three or four rocks in their possession, boom, they sometimes jam them in their mouth and swallow them. If it's an ounce, or even half an ounce, that is way too much dope to put in your body. Very risky. Usually, the crack is in a plastic bag. If that ruptures, it's all over.

Some dope dealers have died as a result of a bag opening in their stomach. The contents hit their bloodstream and they are done.

So that's why the SWAT team, hoping to catch a bunch of sleeping dealers, came banging on my door so early.

As I sat on the couch cuffed, getting more and more anxious while awaiting what was to me an obvious verdict, Rick stood on the other side of the room, talking in a low voice to some of the other officers.

"Get it over with already," I thought.

Finally Rick came back to face me. I felt like I was back in court, facing a judge about to sentence me.

But then, Rick said the six words that proved to be the turning point in my life, the six words I will never forget: "I'm not going to charge you."

My jaw dropped.

"I trust you and I believe in you," Rick said.

I couldn't believe what I was hearing.

I learned later that Boldus had come up to Rick when they were huddled and asked, "You got enough? Can you charge him?"

Rick shook his head. He wasn't ready. He had a feeling in his gut that charging me would be an injustice. Considering how many warrants he had executed, his instincts were excellent. He had learned to study the reaction of suspects, giving him a feel for their guilt or innocence.

"Might I have been wrong on occasion?" he once said to me. "Yeah, but I felt pretty good about my assessment of people."

So finally, after thinking it over a little longer, my life hanging in the balance, Rick decided to go with his gut feeling. He went to the highest-ranking officer of the group, Lieutenant Chris Larson, and told him, "I don't think this kid had any idea the dope was in this house."

Thankfully, Larson said, "I trust you. If you don't feel right about this, I don't want you to do it."

"Well then, that's a done deal," Rick said. "This kid walks."

After he had removed the handcuffs from my wrist, he looked me in the eye and said, "I hope I'm not screwing up on this and I hope you are not involved in dope dealing. If you are, I promise you, you and I will meet again because I'm really good at my job."

I nodded my head, tears welling up in my eyes.

In his nearly three decades as a police officer, Rick never did anything like this, before or since. He did let dealers go on occasion in order to catch bigger fish, telling them, "You are going to call me tomorrow and we are going to work together to find the person who was supplying you with dope." But simply allowing someone caught in my situation to walk away? Never.

As Rick headed out the door, my mom said to him, "I feel sorry for other police officers out there who aren't like you, who don't have a heart, who don't help other young men who were in my son's situation. You know those drugs are not his."

"Yeah, I know that," Rick replied. "If I thought the dope was his, he'd be leaving with me."

When the SWAT team had left, my mom looked upwards and said, "Thank you God for giving him another chance."

"And God bless that detective who believed in you," she told me. "I would have probably died if they took you. At the very least, I wouldn't have had any hair left. It would have just come out from the stress."

In Wisconsin at that time, specifically in Racine County, the term used to describe my situation was "constructed possession." As Rick later explained it to me, "You're in the house. You're in charge of the house. Dope's in the house. The dope is now yours. That was a decision that could be contested in court. But as far as charging a suspect under those circumstances, it happened all the time."

If I had been fifteen or younger when Rick and company came knocking on my door, I would not have been considered the primary resident of the house. But on that January morning, I was seventeen, an adult in their eyes, and I was the only one in the house when they arrived. That should have been enough to put me back behind bars.

There were two other factors that could have made my sentence even harsher. One was the amount of coke found in the garage. According to judicial guidelines for possession with intent, which is what I would have been charged with, anything over fifteen grams moves the defendant to the next level in terms of the length of the sentence. Rick and his crew found 15.3 grams in that drainpipe. Plus our house on Bluff Avenue was only a block and a half from Park High. If you are found in possession of drugs within a thousand feet of a school, that's considered a penalty enhancer. In plain English, more time behind bars.

Bottom line: I would have been looking at a minimum of ten years in prison.

Junebug was still in prison himself when he heard about the raid. He later told me he was surprised to hear they had let me go. I had already been behind bars for selling drugs, and the dope had been found in a house where the only other residents were my mother and my underage brother. I was known by police to be a regular at the 18th Street park, and I had two uncles who had been sent away for selling dope.

"Add it all up," Junebug later told me, "and there's no way you could beat the rap. I would have expected the cops to have said, 'This kid is just the next in line.' Instead, somebody was looking over you. That detective saved your life."

The incident also made Junebug think of Uncle Carlos. "Your uncle," said Junebug, "wasn't lucky enough to have a cop who said, 'I know these aren't your drugs.'"

I understood that the detective who had saved me had put his career on the line to do so. Given this unlikely second chance to make something of my life, there was no way I was going to throw it away. But even if the lure of the neighborhood ever tempted me again, I knew I could be ruining not only my future, but Rick's as well. If I was to go back on the streets and sell drugs or, even worse, kill somebody, his fellow cops would surely tell him, "You caused this because you had a chance to lock him up and you didn't."

I learned later that Rick got support for his decision as soon as he left my house. In the police van driving back to police headquarters, he sat next to Andre Steward, one of the cops who used to lecture me about going straight. "You have no idea how good this kid is on a basketball court, do you?" Dre said.

"No, should I?" replied Rick.

Even though I was having a great season at Park High, had become one of the top basketball players in the state, and had recently been the subject of a feature story in the *Journal Times* about how I had turned my life around, Rick didn't even know I played hoops at Park. He didn't follow high school sports.

"This kid will go pro," Dre told him. "He is that good."

"Good for him," Rick said.

Not everybody approved. Many officers in the Racine Police Department were critical of Rick's decision. Time and again, he heard comments like, "You are going to regret this. He's going to be back slinging dope next week."

Even after all the success I had at UConn and in the NBA, some of those cops refused to change their mind. Their attitude was, once a thug, always a thug.

During the year I was with the Lakers, I did an autograph signing at Regency Mall in Racine. A woman came up to me, paid for the autograph, and said, "Could you make it out to Detective Geller?"

That got my attention. I smiled, gave her the autograph, and said, "You tell him I said thank you so much."

Rick proudly displayed the autograph on his desk at work until one of his superiors came over, a frown on his face, and said, "Put it away."

I didn't see Rick again for ten years after he left my house that morning, but now, we have a good relationship. He's always looking out for me.

One night, long after I had turned pro, I was in a club with my brother, and he got into a confrontation with a couple of guys.

Concerned about his safety and anxious to avoid seeing this scene played out in the media, I grabbed Junior and the friends we were with and got out of there. The troublemakers who had gotten in Junior's face followed.

As we moved quickly down the street, up ahead, I spotted the last thing I wanted to see in this situation, a squad car parked by the curb. But then, my concern melted as I saw the officer who was getting out of the car: Rick Geller.

"Can you just let me get my brother home safe?" I yelled as I ran by.

"I got you, Bud. Go," said Rick without hesitation.

As we passed him, six guys came charging out of the bar. When they saw him standing in the middle of the sidewalk ahead of them, they stopped, looked at each other, then turned and grudgingly returned to the bar and their beer.

Once, through one of his informants, Rick learned that a gang on the south side had discussed how nice it would be to take me out, kill a big NBA star. If the opportunity presented itself, they were serious about shooting me.

Since I was living and playing in another city, Rick called my mom and told her, "I don't want to alarm you. This is what's being said . . . Tell Caron to be careful."

For a while after that, when I was home, I didn't wander around Racine alone.

Now the relationship goes beyond just me and Rick. Every time he runs into my mother, who he calls "a great lady," or my grandmother, who he refers to as "a sweetheart," they hug. "I can't say enough good about your mother," Rick has told me, "and what she did to keep you on the right path."

I follow his son, Sawyer, on Twitter. I have a unique bond with Sawyer because he was born eleven days after Rick raided my house and gave me the break of my life.

Throughout the season, Rick will send me texts, congratulating me if I did well and telling me to put it behind me if I had a bad game. That means a lot to me, especially when things aren't going well, for him to take the time to show his support.

He once told a reporter, "I am so grateful that my heart led me in the right direction when I entered that house. The good that has come out of it is amazing. I can take credit for one small decision. Everything else is on him."

For me, it was much more than a small decision. It was a game changer.

What impresses me most about Rick is that he didn't set me free because he knew I was a rising basketball star and that he could share in the glory if I was successful. He didn't know about my potential. He didn't even know I played basketball. All he knew was that I was a kid who looked like he was agonizing over being in the wrong place at the wrong time. So he did the right thing.

And for that, I will always respect him.

THIRTEEN

MY TIME WITH MAD MAX: GENTRY, MCI, AND A WHOLE NEW WORLD

It was time.

Deep down, I knew it and my mother knew it.

Time to put Racine in my rearview mirror and find an environment where I could fulfill my potential. There wasn't always going to be a Rick Geller around to save me.

Even my old P.E. teacher, Jim Betker, told me, "You have the ability, but you've got to get yourself out of here."

Still, for a while, I was in denial. I didn't want to leave the only home I had ever known, the place where I was born and raised, the place where I had my whole family, my friends, the people I trusted. So I fought the reality of my situation. I knew, considering all the honors I had won playing basketball for Park High, that school officials would do everything possible to keep me.

The issue was eligibility. My high school eligibility started the second I walked into Case High. I was only there for about thirty days, shipped off to jail before Halloween of that first semester. The clock, however, kept ticking for me. Even though I didn't even get a chance to take part in a sport at Case, even though I was behind bars, the time was considered part of my eligibility period.

By the time I enrolled at Park High, I had already missed my freshman and sophomore years. When I played a full season there, it was as a junior.

So I should have still had another year. Instead, I was told that my eligibility had run out. Park High officials appealed to the Wisconsin Interscholastic Athletic Association, but the request was denied.

Looking back, that was a blessing. But at the time, I felt lost, unwanted. What was I going to do? I had won every basketball award I possibly could in my first season of high school competition, yet there I was, back on the street, my eligibility denied.

Damn, what next?

Fortunately, my grades were decent and I had already grown to 6'7", the same height I am today. I was playing for Jameel's traveling AAU squad, and he was the one who first put the idea in my head of going to a prep school, a private school that prepares students for college.

I needed to find the right coach at the right school, a place that would accept my remaining eligibility. But I didn't know anything about prep schools, where they were, how you got in, how much they cost.

Because of the name I had made for myself at Park High, I was invited to play in a high-profile basketball tournament in the South. I knew it was high-profile when I saw coaches like Mike Krzyzewski and Jim Calhoun sitting in the stands watching *me*.

That shouldn't have surprised me. I was one of the top high school small forwards in the country. Then, I was invited to play in a prep tournament in Indiana where I was named one of the top five players at the event.

All of this exposure had to pay off. I was a player with height and skills who could compete at a national level and still had some eligibility remaining, a big fish coming out of a small pond. Somebody was going to stick their rod in the water to reel me in.

Somebody did, Max Good, the basketball coach at Maine Central Institute in Pittsfield, Maine.

When he first called, after hearing about me, he was Mad Max.

The first thing he said to me was, "You motherfucker."

That was before he even said hello.

"This program is the best in the country," Max told me. "I don't need your ass. You come here, you'd better have your shit together, put away all your scrapbooks and be ready to work."

That didn't scare me.

Then he gave me the bad news. Annual tuition was $17,000.

I told him there was no way I had that kind of money.

Max said he was willing to take me in on a scholarship, but that would still cost me $5,500 for the school year.

I told him I didn't even have that much money.

"Get it," Max said.

Click.

He sounded like a mean old man, but my mom and I realized this was my road to salvation. It was time to go and now I had a destination. I had to find the money.

I may have been out of the dope game by then, but I knew plenty of people who were still in it. For them, $5,500 was less than a week's work.

First, I asked a cousin who was hustling in the streets and doing quite well, bringing in the kind of big bucks I used to make. He said to come over to his house, and he would give me the money.

I went over there several times, but he was never home. Was he ducking me? I didn't have time to find out.

So I went to another drug dealer, a guy named Jamie Harris, and told him my situation. He knew me, knew my story, and was a friend of my family. I told him I needed $5,500, but "could really use a little cushion, maybe $6,000 to $7,000 just to be on the safe side."

"I gotcha," he said. "When do you need it by?" "Shit," I told him, "I need it like yesterday."

Jamie drove me to his house and gave me the money that quick. Respect is due him for the way he stepped up and backed me when my future was on the line.

Unfortunately, his drug dealing caught up with him and he got ten years in prison. I would go visit him all the time in Terre Haute, Indiana, where he was imprisoned, even after I got into the NBA. I always looked out for him, made sure he was doing well because he took care of me, gave me the needed push to start me on the path I'm still traveling today.

As for the money, I paid Jamie back ten times over.

He is still my friend to this day. He just got out of jail and we kick it all the time.

It was tough to say goodbye to everybody, especially my mom and my grandma, but there was no turning back at that point. Even my mom, who had not wanted me to even move to Milwaukee when I was younger, admitted moving halfway across the country was the best thing for me. The stress of knowing someone might kill me at any time, anywhere in town, was killing her.

"You've got to get out of here," she told me.

I packed everything I needed into four big luggage bags and headed for the airport in Milwaukee for an early-morning departure, the first of four flights that day that would get me to Bangor, Maine.

I went from Milwaukee to Chicago, Chicago to Boston, and then two shorter flights to reach Bangor. It took all day and a good chunk of the night. By the time I got off the last plane, it was coming up on midnight.

My first thought was about food. Because the flights were so close together, and unfamiliar with different airports and travel procedures, I barely made some of them. I never had a chance to eat in the fifteen hours since I had left Racine.

The terminal at Bangor International Airport was largely deserted when I arrived. The few restaurants there were closed.

Dragging my four bags, I spotted a little old white man near the street entrance with a big Airedale dog named, as I soon learned, Gentry.

It had to be Max. There was nobody else around.

"How you doing?" he said without introducing himself.

I put my hand out to shake his, but he kept his hands at his side.

"How are you doing, sir?" I said, ignoring the slight.

"Don't sir me," Max replied. "How many bags you got?"

"Four."

"Alright, get your shit and go out there," he said, pointing to the street. "I'll be in the van."

I'm thinking, "You're not going to help me?"

It took me several trips to get all my luggage.

"Hurry up," said Max on my third trip back into the terminal.

I finally got all the bags into the van, got in myself, and off we went.

Looking around in the dark as we drove, I didn't see any lights anywhere. It was so pitch black that it was hard to see much of anything beyond the highway.

"There ain't nothing to do out here," I said.

"You want me to take your ass back to the airport?" said Max, his voice rising. "Oh, you have so much to do in Racine?"

I knew I didn't want to go home, so I shut the hell up.

We traveled about fifteen miles, and then, I saw up ahead the most wonderful sight I could imagine at that moment. I was like a wanderer in the desert, dying of thirst and suddenly seeing a pool of water. Only in my case, starving like hell, what I saw, appearing through the darkness, was the golden arches.

McDonald's!!

Were we going to stop? Yes! Max pulled into the drive-thru lane, rolled his window down, and stopped at the speaker box where orders are placed.

I was sitting in the passenger seat with Gentry between Max and me, his paws on the console box, his head on his paws, his eyes looking straight ahead.

"You want something, boy?" Max asked.

"Yeah," I said, "I want a No. 2 . . ."

"I ain't talking to your ass."

He was talking to the *dog*.

Gentry growled and Max ordered a Big Mac.

When it came, he unwrapped it, tossed it on the floor of the van, and Gentry jumped down and gobbled it up in two bites. He looked up at me and licked his lips.

I'm thinking, "Did this motherfucker just feed this dog and not feed me?"

Yep.

With my stomach growling louder than Gentry, we took off for Pittsfield. About twenty minutes later, we reached Maine Central Institute.

I dragged my bags out, Max and Gentry just watching as if they didn't even know me, and we walked into a building that turned out to be a two-story dorm.

Max flipped on the lights, waking up all the boys, both upstairs and downstairs.

"Everybody put your clothes on," he yelled. "We are going to the gym."

It was about one o'clock in the morning by then.

I could hear the grumbling from all sides on both floors.

"Everybody shut the fuck up," shouted Max, "or you are going to be running all night."

The complaining was reduced to low muttering and then it was quiet as sheets and blankets were thrown off and the boys, rubbing their eyes and shaking their heads, began to pull out jerseys, shorts, socks, and shoes.

I dropped my luggage, reached into the bag where I kept my gear, and began to suit up myself.

"I can't believe this," I thought. "Am I ever going to eat?"

Not right then. Max marched everybody out into the cold night and over to the gym, where he announced we were going to have a five-on-five scrimmage.

"Shirts and skins," he said. "Jump ball."

Somehow, despite the exhaustion and the hunger pangs, I found my legs and my shot and got into the flow of the game. I dunked. Dunked again.

"We don't do that shit here," said Max.

I was definitely beginning to feel comfortable, because I even got into a yelling match with one of the other players. It became real intense real fast.

Max came over, told us both to cool it, and then announced that the scrimmage was over.

Everybody shuffled off back to bed leaving just me, Max, and Gentry in the gym. For the first time since I had met him a couple of hours earlier, Max smiled.

"I just wanted to make sure you were worth the trouble of keeping you here," he said.

I, too, smiled, then followed my new teammates back to the dorm, found an empty bed, curled up eighteen hours after I had left Racine, and that's the last thing I remember until morning.

Even if I could have found some food, I was too tired by then to even eat.

But breakfast the next morning sure tasted good. Even better than a Big Mac.

For a poor kid from the south side of Racine, coming to Pittsfield, population a little over three thousand, and attending Maine Central was like landing on another planet.

From a crime-ridden area where it was advisable to always carry a weapon when going out at night, I found myself in a town where people slept with their front doors unlocked and their keys dangling in their parked cars.

The whole town was only about three blocks long. The local movie theater had about thirty seats and showed films that were three to five years old. I got to see deer and moose for the first time.

When my teammates and I did our grocery shopping, we got our supplies at a gas station that took IOUs if you didn't have the money. If the customers were townspeople who the proprietors knew, they would let the customers simply walk out with their purchases along with a promise to pay on Friday when they got their paycheck.

For someone like me, who had seen more robberies than I could count, it was awkward at first. I kept thinking there had to be a catch, that maybe it was a trick to frame me for a crime. But I soon learned that there was no ulterior motive behind the generous spirit of the Pittsfield townspeople. It was just a different attitude, a different way of life.

All but two of the members of the MCI basketball team were black, but we didn't run into any blatant prejudice in Pittsfield. Townspeople would joke that, during basketball season, the African-American population in Pittsfield would skyrocket, but I didn't sense any malice behind that remark.

On the contrary, the town took us in, enabling us to leave the campus and stay with host families on the weekends when there was no conflict with our basketball schedule.

For the two years I was at MCI, I had the same host family, Deborah McKay, the school nurse, and her three kids.

Deborah was going through a divorce at the time and her soon-to-be ex-husband had moved to the family's lake house. Deborah got the big house in Pittsfield, and that's where I stayed. One of her daughters, Megan, was an MCI graduate who was a freshman in college by the time I moved in, so she was only home part of the time. But Deborah's other daughter, Katie, was in my grade at MCI. The oldest of Deborah's kids was a boy named Raul.

Deborah took good care of me, bought me things, fed me, gave me my own room, and even let me take off in her car when I wanted a little freedom. Being on campus at MCI, she was able to keep an eye on me and make sure I didn't extend my desire for freedom to class time.

The whole family accepted me with open arms. The atmosphere in the household was totally foreign to me, but very warm and comfortable. We would do everything together, sit down to dinner, watch TV, play checkers or board games like Monopoly, crack jokes, and laugh a lot.

It was like what I had seen in those old TV sitcoms I had watched in Racine, thinking back then that such a lifestyle was just make-believe, convinced people didn't really live like that.

Staying in the McKay house, I even started watching the news channels like CNN and learning about the world around me for the first time, something I would have never thought of doing in Racine.

Once I was exposed to everything offered by that town, that campus, and that household, I began thinking differently. I guess that's the idea behind prep school.

MCI itself was different than any other school I had ever seen. It was an old, old institution, built in 1866 in a sheep pasture. In the beginning, it had a total of thirty-two students and classes were taught in private homes, public halls, and the village schoolhouse. Today MCI has approximately 450 students, fifty full-time teachers along with part-timers, thirty coaches, an administrative staff of eleven, and a support staff of around thirty. The campus, tree-lined and beautiful, has six classroom buildings, four residence halls, and two gyms.

For seventy years, MCI was known for its award-winning rifle team. But then, along came Max.

He was a coaching legend in Maine when I joined the team for what would be his tenth and, as it turned out, last season as coach of the MCI Huskies. He finished with a 275-30 record for a .902 winning percentage that included three undefeated teams and five New England Prep School Athletic Conference championships.

Max got the town's attention from the start, his first team at MCI finishing 26-0 in 1989–1990, followed by a 24-0 record the following season. He actually lost a game in his third year after winning his first seventy-nine games with the Huskies, the 1991-1992 squad suffering a defeat in its final game to wind up 29-1.

Over the years, 135 of his players, including me, went on to play Division I basketball, and ten, including me, made it to the NBA. Among the latter group were Sam Cassell, Cuttino Mobley, Brad Miller, and Der-Marr Johnson.

I was accustomed to joining a basketball program and immediately making it better. That wasn't necessary at MCI. When I first suited up, Max already had the Huskies in the midst of another phenomenal run. The team had been 35-0 the previous season.

I could immediately see why he had been so successful. He was a great coach, one of the best I've ever seen. Max had coached at Eastern

Kentucky University for eight seasons before coming to MCI. He had been offered opportunities to return to the collegiate level, but had turned them down because he liked building a program with prep kids, and he liked having the total control he enjoyed at Maine Central.

The first thing I noticed was the tight structure of his program. He appreciated talent. He didn't appreciate attitude. Since I had both, I knew we were going to bang heads at some point. And I wasn't going to get the final word. Compared to Max, Jameel had been soft. And I had lost the battle of wills with him.

Once we started scrimmaging, I realized Max had been serious when he had told me on the phone that he could get along without me. Everybody on the team was Division I ready. We had DerMarr, the No. 1 high school player in the country. We had Wesley Wilson, 6'11", 250 pounds, one of the top ten high school centers in the nation, and Avery Queen, a top ten guard. Under Max, I developed into a top prep player. We were stacked. Max recruited hard and got the best.

I was excited when he put me in the starting lineup right away, playing either power forward or center, but I had a lot to learn.

I had been playing streetball my whole life, but Max taught me how the X's and O's of the game could be put into a structure. I learned a lot about preparation from him, about discipline, about playing with others, about sacrificing. And I learned what it took to win a championship. He had created a winning culture at MCI and it was infectious. Either you caught the spirit or you were gone.

Before I got to Maine, I had just wanted to be the best showman on the court. My attitude was, "Shit, I can play. It ain't my fault the other guys on this team can't play."

Now it was, "How can I make those around me better? How can I be an asset to my team?"

At times, I slipped into my old habits, playing my game rather than playing within the system. I still had some rebel in me.

Max would look at me and say, "There you go again with that streetball shit."

"I'm sorry," I would say. "I'm working on it."

When something works for you from the first day you step on a basketball court, it's kind of tough when somebody says, "Stop doing that." I would eventually stop, but it was a process.

Fortunately I had the right coach to guide me through the transformation. Max was willing to work with me because, as he told others, "Caron has an edge when he plays. I like that about him."

One time in practice, I was jogging up the court, doing my little trot.

That got Max upset. He yelled at me, "You can do much better than that. Why don't you just sit down. You obviously don't want to run today. You ain't doing shit."

That got my attention. When he allowed me back on the court, I started accelerating like Carl Lewis. From that point on, I was running in drills harder than everybody else, flying up and down the court, barreling people over.

Finally, Max said, "Alright, you can slow your ass down."

I liked that he challenged me. He challenged DerMarr. He challenged all of us to be the best that we could possibly be. He wouldn't let us settle for mediocrity.

He told us so in no uncertain terms. As a matter of fact, Max told us everything in no uncertain terms.

You never had to wonder where you stood with him. He said what he thought and didn't play mind games. He was an honest cat.

When Max was upset during a game, he would stomp around on the sideline. In the locker room, he would throw chairs or kick them à la Bobby Knight.

As a result of his tirades, Max broke his hand at least four times that I know of and once broke his foot. One time, he smacked the blackboard so hard while discussing a play we had messed up that he split his hand open. Blood was running down his shirt and onto his pants, but he just kept talking, kept swinging his arms. Guys were ducking to avoid getting sprayed. He was always trying so hard to get his message across that his delivery was like no other.

Yeah, he'd get crazy, but he'd get us crazy too, and that was his plan. He was an animated coach, passionate, very emotional.

If Max felt recruiters were stepping over the line and becoming a distraction, he'd kick them out. He didn't care.

He wasn't just tough when it came to basketball. He was just as demanding about academics. MCI officials regarded us as *student-*athletes, emphasis on the student part. Max abided by that philosophy, maintaining an academics-first atmosphere around the basketball program.

It wasn't easy for me. Prior to coming to Maine, my grades were C's and D's. When I got to MCI, I found the bar for academic standards very high. There were no administrators willing to give athletes bogus courses so we could concentrate on our sport, no teachers willing to look the other way if we missed class.

School officials loved what we accomplished on the court, but wouldn't consider easing our classroom workload so that we could devote more time and effort to athletics.

I understood that. School is school. So I would stay after class, I would come early. To help us, Max organized study groups for his players. We would meet at MCI for up to two and a half hours per session. School officials even took the pay phone off the hook in the hallway so there would be no distractions, no excuse for not keeping our heads in our textbooks.

My favorite subject was history. I loved learning about America's past and how our culture evolved. It's always important to know where you came from to help you figure out where you're headed.

No matter how well we did, however, academically or athletically, we would never get any kudos from Max. He didn't want us to get overconfident and cocky. He would praise us to our families and school officials. But to our face, he would bash us. "Oh, you ain't shit," he would say. "You think you are good, don't you?"

One time, my mom told me, "I talked to Max and he said you are doing great in school."

I said, "Excuse me, what Max did you talk to? I never heard him say anything good about me."

That's when I knew he really cared about me and my teammates. He wanted only the best for us.

And that's why I loved Coach. I learned something from him every day, about basketball or life.

Besides Max, there were other things to like about MCI. I made some good friends there. I was able to talk freely about my checkered past without having people look down on me.

But there were times I felt lonely, feelings neither Max nor my friends nor the McKays could soothe. I missed home. I missed my mom and my grandma and all my family and old friends. In the two years I was at MCI, I only got home twice a semester.

And my mom couldn't afford to come east to Pittsfield. It was a love/hate situation for her. While she felt the same loneliness I did every time she walked by my bedroom at home, she loved the fact that I was in a better place.

She still worked all those jobs and all those crazy hours to pay the rent and her bills and support my kid brother. In addition, she had to pay the huge phone bills I racked up with all my long-distance calls from Maine (sure would have loved to have had a cell phone back then), she sent me money weekly, and she paid $100 a month in child support to Danisha for Camary.

My mom had too much pride to borrow money to come see me, and too much fear that she would never be able to pay it back. She did scrape enough together to come to Pittsfield one time for a brief visit, but she wasn't there long enough to attend a game.

The low point was my graduation. I had nobody there when I went up for my diploma.

We finished 34-4 in my first season at MCI and won the conference championship. Given my high-profile role on a high-profile prep school program, I found myself the focus of recruiters from many of the top universities.

But just when I had finally found myself in the position I had dreamed of, I lost the person I had come to depend on the most to get me there. After years of fighting off the college folks, Max gave in and accepted a job at UNLV as an assistant coach. He went on to become head coach there for one season and spent seven seasons as head coach at Bryant University in Smithfield, Rhode Island, and six seasons coaching Loyola Marymount. He is now back at UNLV as special assistant to head coach Dave Rice.

Max may have cut his connection to MCI, but our connection remains to this day. He never lets up, still getting on me even now when I deserve it.

During the time he was head coach at Loyola, I spent a season with the Clippers, living only a couple of blocks from him. I would go to his games to support him or meet him for dinner on a regular basis.

Old Gentry wasn't around anymore, so I didn't have to worry about having nothing to eat.

FOURTEEN

COLLEGE: UCONN AND ANDREA, THE LOVE OF MY LIFE

When I was a kid playing streetball and hanging out at the Bryant Center, I never thought about college. I wasn't exactly living in a Brady Bunch neighborhood, and I figured that was the kind of life you had to have to be admitted to college. I thought you had to be special.

Besides, my goal back then was to play in the NBA. The way I saw it as a naïve youngster, you became a good player, the NBA coaches heard about you, came knocking on your door, and said, "We need you."

So, when I became the best on the south side of Racine, I was confused, thinking, "Why haven't they come for me?"

There are many communities across America where young people don't know how to become successful because they haven't been exposed to role models who made it to the top. In the minds of those young people, and I include myself in that group, the road to success didn't come through their town.

But despite the frustration, I remained a dreamer. I thought I could be anything I wanted to be.

The idea first began to creep into my head that my dreams really could come true during practice days toward the end of my first year at MCI. When I looked around the gym, I started seeing some familiar faces, like those of Jim Calhoun, coach of UConn, then the defending NCAA champions, John Thompson of Georgetown, Gene Keady of Purdue, and John Chaney of Temple along with a bunch of assistant coaches and scouts.

Those were coaches I had seen on TV and now, damn, they were right there, so close I could step off the court and touch them.

I was in awe.

Then I got goose bumps when coaches actually started talking to me, telling me, "I would love to have you play for me."

Caron Butler from the south side playing for Jim Calhoun or John Thompson? That didn't seem real. I knew I had talent, and now I had people reinforcing my belief in my skill level, important people.

The first coach to tell me he wanted me to sign a letter of intent was Karl Hobbs, one of Coach Calhoun's assistants. Once UConn made the first move, others jumped into the pool as well. Duke, St. John's, Georgetown, and Marquette also expressed interest in me. The competition to get me was growing fierce and I loved it. Instead of cops chasing me, I now had big-time coaches after me.

My talent was certainly an attraction, but so was the coach already in my corner. Those who were recruiting me knew, if you've been coached by Max Good, you know the game of basketball. Those other coaches knew I had been drilled on staying consistent night in and night out, on the importance of maintaining my professionalism on the court, on working as hard in practice as I worked in a game. When college coaches signed a graduate of MCI in those days, they could be confident they were going to get a well-trained prospect.

I thought UConn would be the place for me because of the success Richard Hamilton and Ray Allen, players similar to me, had enjoyed under Coach Calhoun. I felt like I could step in and fill their roles. Coach Calhoun ran a system that fit me and I could fulfill my potential in it.

But before I put my signature on a letter of intent, I flirted with two other colleges. Actually, it was more than a flirtation. I verbally committed to two other schools.

When Keady came after me, I couldn't resist the chance to play at the alma mater of Glenn Robinson, my favorite player. So I gave a verbal commitment to Purdue.

Everybody who wined and dined me (just kidding, NCAA) dangled something appealing in front of me. Hobbs talked to me about the importance of family at UConn.

He hit the right button. Being in a tight family unit back home in Racine and missing it when I first got to Maine, then having it again with the McKays, I liked the idea of experiencing it once again in college.

"You need to come to UConn for a visit," Hobbs told me, "and see how family oriented we are and what we are building there."

In the summer after my first year at MCI, I made recruiting trips to UConn, Purdue, and Marquette. While I was at Connecticut, Coach Calhoun arranged for me to meet some of his big-name players, current and former, all of whom put pressure on me to sign. It was gentle, but convincing pressure.

Khalid El-Amin, who had helped UConn win its first NCAA championship just a few months earlier, Kevin Ollie, currently the Huskies' head coach, Cliff Robinson and Scott Burrell, both members of the UConn Basketball All-Century Team and both of whom went on to the NBA, all talked to me.

That was impressive.

I watched Ollie, Robinson, and Burrell play in a pickup game.

That was also impressive.

But I think what really stuck in my mind was my conversation with Allen, who was the fifth pick in the 1996 NBA Draft out of UConn and was playing for the Milwaukee Bucks, my hometown team, at the time.

"If you want to be great, this is the place to come," Ray told me. "If you want to be in a system where you are going to be highlighted, be able to play the game you love at a high level, and be challenged, this is where you want to play."

By then, Max had been hired by UNLV as an assistant under head coach Bill Bayno. Maybe the Runnin' Rebels added Max to their staff because they thought it would cause me to follow him to Vegas. That I did, but it was only for a visit. I wasn't staying. I went there out of respect for Max, but I had pretty much made up my mind to take advantage of the opportunity to begin my college career playing for the defending NCAA champs.

Any lingering doubts faded when I went home to Racine that summer and Coach Calhoun followed me.

I was playing a pickup game at the Bryant Center and in he walked. He didn't say anything, just sat down and watched.

I could hear the buzz spreading around the gym. "That's Coach Calhoun of the champion Huskies," people whispered.

There was even a story in the *Journal Times*: "Jim Calhoun is in Racine, Wisconsin."

My friends were telling me, "If Jim Calhoun came all the way out here, you've got to go to Connecticut."

After I got done playing that day, he and I talked.

"I would love to have you," Coach Calhoun told me. "I know you have dreams of going to the NBA and doing all sorts of great things. I'm telling you, the University of Connecticut is the best place for you to make your dreams come true, to make everything happen.

"It's going to be hard. There's going to be competition. I'm not giving you any guarantees about playing time, but I will guarantee you that you will be the best Caron Butler that you possibly can be at the University of Connecticut."

That's all I needed to hear. It was a challenge, but it was also the opportunity for stability and family.

And it came from a coach I felt I could trust. He didn't kiss my ass. He didn't give me the sales pitch so many coaches toss at recruits. They will tell a player they are trying to sign, "You the man. You will start. It's all about you." Then they will tell another player, "I don't know about the last guy I was talking to, but it's about you."

Coaches like that turn me off. If you can be bought, you can be sold.

"Do you believe in yourself?" he asked me. "I know that you may be one of the top prep players in the country. I get it, but you've still got to work and I'm going to push you. Do you want that?"

I looked at him and said, "Where do I sign?"

I was nineteen years old.

Both coaches, Calhoun and Hobbs, spoke to my mom on the phone. She didn't know anything about basketball or the best college for me. She was just happy all these schools were offering me a free education. She was making $22,000 a year, and I was going to go to college tuition free. To her, that was unbelievable.

I had a press conference at the George Bray Neighborhood Center to announce my future destination, but it would have to remain in the future. My academic standing was not yet sufficient to get me into Connecticut. So I was going to have to go back to MCI for one more year, my fifth year of high school, to finish my classes. Fortunately, the MCI basketball team was part of a post-graduate program, meaning players who had used up their high school eligibility, like me, could still compete.

It wasn't the same for me at MCI after Max left, even though I had better numbers in my second season. As team captain under new coach Karl Henrikson, I averaged 26 points and 13 rebounds after averaging 19 points and 12 rebounds the year before. This time, in our bid for the conference championship, we got only as far as the semifinals before being eliminated.

Then, it was time for me to move on.

When I first arrived at UConn, my life immediately changed forever.

And it had nothing to do with basketball.

During the summer before school started, I enrolled in a precollegiate program for minority students run by CAP (Center for Academic Programs). It was a chance to get a head start on earning credits and to also get a feel of the campus and the academic workload. There were about one hundred in the group, three of us athletes.

There was also a New Haven, Connecticut, girl named Andrea Pink, whose family had migrated from Jamaica before she was born. We were in a couple of classes together, but our relationship at that point basically consisted of saying hi and nodding to each other in the hallway.

I later found out that her first impression of me was pretty low. She would look out her dorm window and see me with a crowd around me, talking loud, cracking jokes, having a good time. She thought I was just seeking attention.

Andrea prefers to sit back and observe, so I rubbed her the wrong way.

Not knowing anything about sports, she didn't realize that all the attention was coming my way unsolicited because I was a hot new recruit on a basketball team that had captured the imagination of the campus, not to mention basketball fans across the country. Once Andrea realized I just had an outgoing personality and being the big man on campus was unavoidable for me as a Huskies basketball player, her attitude softened.

The academic program was tougher than anything I was going to face on the court. We spent six weeks, ending in July, housed in dorms and taking classes in math, science, and English from 9:00 in the morning to 10:00 at night.

Tough as it was, it turned out to be a good experience. It gave me a taste of campus life, allowed me to make friends with students who weren't connected to the basketball team, expanding my view of college, and it resulted in the formation of study groups that would help me keep my grades up and stay eligible.

It was, however, a tough time for Andrea. A serious student straight out of high school, she resented the fact that this special program had been created just for minority students.

"I honestly think they brought us here," she later told me, "thinking we weren't going to achieve as well as the white students without some extra help."

Andrea felt even deeper resentment toward the college when one of her grandmothers, Joyce, her mother's mother, passed away in Jamaica during that six-week session.

Her whole family was going back to Jamaica for the funeral, but when Andrea asked college officials if she could take a brief leave of absence from the six-week program, she was told that wouldn't be possible. If she left the precollegiate program, they said, she would lose her spot at the university once the regular semester began.

So while her mother, Shirley, her sister, Kasia, and other family members left to join her father, Earl, who had previously moved back to Jamaica, and other mourners in their homeland, Andrea had to stay behind.

Looking back, she realized what she had been told wasn't accurate. She had already been accepted by the college, and missing part of a precollegiate program would not have disqualified her.

"I never forgave them for that," Andrea has told me.

Coming to UConn as a nursing major before switching to Human Development and Family Studies, she moved back into the dorm for the start of her freshman year.

Making a decision she quickly came to regret, Andrea accepted an invitation from an RA (residence aide stationed in the dorms to help students) to come to his dorm room to watch a movie, a common activity between RAs and students all over campus.

But this time was horribly different. Andrea had to fight off the guy when he tried to attack her. She escaped, thank God, without being harmed.

When she got back to her room, Andrea immediately called her sister. Kasia immediately came to the campus and went with her sister to report the incident to college officials. Andrea declined, however, to press charges because her mother would have then been informed and Andrea knew what that would mean. She would be ordered to come home and forget about UConn.

School officials insisted that she at least go to counseling, and they moved her to another dorm, away from where that RA was living.

Andrea never saw him again and assumed he was kicked out of UConn.

The good news was, she was moved to the building next to mine, our windows facing each other. We spoke periodically from that vantage point, and if she was going out for food, she would occasionally bring me something as well.

It was the start of a beautiful relationship.

Before I even put on a UConn uniform, I was approached by officials from the NCAA who were investigating how urban athletes like me got the money to go to prep schools like Maine Central Institute.

In my case, my $600 deposit to MCI to hold a spot open was paid by the Bray Center in Racine, a nonprofit 501(c)(3) organization, meaning it had tax-exempt status.

As I mentioned earlier, I got the tuition money from Jamie Harris, a drug dealer who was a friend of mine and the rest of my family. When the NCAA investigators asked me where the money came from, I said, "The streets."

"We feel like a booster from Connecticut helped you," one investigator told me.

"The man I got the money from," I insisted, "just got convicted in a drug deal and he's facing ten years in prison. That's the truth. I don't know any boosters from Connecticut. I just got here. I don't know anybody."

The NCAA investigators ultimately concluded that I was telling the truth, but they still suspended me for the first three games of the season for accepting the money from Jamie.

I understood. Rules are rules. But it didn't seem like a fair rule. It wasn't like I took the money to get drugs. I took it to further my education. Should I have asked Jamie for financial help? A lot of good things in my life came out of that decision.

Good thing I only took the money from a drug dealer. If it had come from a booster, I would have been in real trouble.

The NCAA championship won by UConn had attracted an incredibly talented recruiting class for my freshman season. We had Taliek Brown, the best guard in New York City, Scott Hazelton, one of the top high school forwards in the country and my chief rival for a starting spot, along with guard Robert Swain and swingman Shamon Tooles.

At first, the biggest change for me was assuming responsibility for myself and my new obligations.

Like getting up with the sun to go running.

In the past, going back to my mom at home, the guards at Ethan Allen, and Max at MCI, I always had somebody on me, yelling at me to get out of bed for some reason or other. Now it was just me, my alarm clock, and my roommate, Taliek.

It was our choice to wake up and get with the program or turn over and face the wrath of Coach Calhoun. I was an adult now. Taliek and I learned to depend on ourselves, pushing and challenging each other.

After a couple of exhibition games and one against Quinnipiac University at the Hartford Civic Center to start the season, we were going to play in the Maui Invitational in Hawaii. And if that wasn't enough pressure, the games would be televised nationally.

We had nine weeks to gear up. We spent it running, training, running, learning the Husky system, and running again. At first, all that running was a bit spooky because the long, winding trail we used passed the tombstones on Cemetery Hill near UConn. The tombstones are everywhere you look. But I wasn't intimidated because I was focused on the thought that I was following in the footsteps of every player who had ever suited up for the Huskies.

After getting up at around 6:30 every morning, we had to be on that hill at 7:15 to begin the first of twelve trips up and down. It would take an hour to an hour and a half.

Then it was time for weight training, then off to class, then basketball practice, then into a study group for academics, then, if I was lucky, a little time for my social life.

Next day, right back to the tombstones to kick off another morning.

All that conditioning and we hadn't even started playing games yet.

I had been a basketball player since I could walk, but this was the first time it involved a formal training program. In the past, I would just walk into a gym and start shooting. Even Max, who had a training program of his own, didn't have a routine like the one designed by Coach Calhoun and his assistants.

Once the games began, I had to prepare for them while also working out a schedule with my professors for assignments I would miss when the team was traveling. Those professors weren't the least bit sympathetic. Even though the basketball programs for both men and women brought much acclaim to the university, many of the teachers considered the players privileged. So they challenged us.

I would be told, "We are not going to just let you turn in half-assed work on your assignments or not be in my class when I know you got in at one o'clock last night and my class is at eight. I expect you here front and center."

If I or one of my teammates were late, the professors would make a huge deal out of it. The spotlight was always on us.

Going to Hawaii for the games in Maui was a great experience for someone like me who had never been to a place like that before. It was unbelievable, from flying first class on the plane to the huge dinners to knowing the cameras would be on me, the whole country able to watch.

Back home, people on the south side of Racine were asking, "Can he play on that level?"

When I called home the day before my first game, my grandmother told me, "We'll be watching you tomorrow."

I replied, "I'm ready."

My grandmother had given me her cell phone to take with me. Because it was before there were cell phone plans, I charged her bill up into the stratosphere, something I'm still sorry for to this day.

I couldn't help myself. I was calling all of my family and friends, wide-eyed as I told them, "Man, there's palm trees out here," or "There are no mosquitos. I haven't gotten bit even though I've got no shirt on."

One person asked, "Where's Hawaii at? Can you drive there?"

"Man, we are on a fucking island," I told him.

My first Maui tournament game, against Louisville, was a special moment for me. Aware of the fact that all my family and friends back home in Racine were watching, I was nervous, but excited. I wanted to prove wrong all the doubters who had said I'd never be anything but a drug dealer and a thug, but I also wanted to stay humble, respecting the occasion. Those thoughts were racing through my mind at the tipoff, but I was determined to put them aside and just go out there and play as hard as I could for as long as I could.

That was my mind-set. And that's what I did. Coach Calhoun put me in about six minutes into the game and I quickly showed my value. The first time I shot the ball, I hit a three-pointer. My second shot was a power dunk. I finished with 20 points and 6 rebounds and we won, 83–71.

I knew after that night that I was going to be all right at the Division I level, but it would take the same type of effort I had expended in that first game, replicated every night, to keep up with the players I would be facing. I showed I could jump, fly around the court, and always be in the spot where Coach Calhoun wanted me because of how seriously I had trained. Along with my physical fitness, I had prepared myself mentally, enabling me to feel comfortable and confident when I was on the court.

But I didn't try to fool myself into thinking I had arrived. It was just the beginning, a good start on which to improve.

When I got back to the hotel, I called my grandmother's house. She had left her front door open for the game and a crowd from the neighborhood had come in to watch on her big-screen TV and cheer along with family members. It was standing room only.

My mom and grandmother were the cheerleaders. My mom jumped up and down during the game, yelling, "That's my baby!"

"If I could have done a backflip," she later told me, "I would have."

I could hear the joy in the air when I called. Several people leaned into the phone to scream, "You did it!"

As I soon learned with the season underway, piling up numbers without adding a higher number to the win column would not get me any praise from Coach Calhoun. He was a hard-nosed leader, just like Max, but even worse. Coach Calhoun was big on structure, detail, a master motivator who made great locker room speeches. He definitely knew how to push players' buttons.

One time, he came in after I had struggled on the court, got in my face, and said, "You going to let those fuckers kick your ass? Are you a man or what?"

I'm thinking, "You questioning my manhood?"

Thinking it, but not daring to say anything.

Coach Calhoun knew how to get you to a place where you would push your body to the limit, pour out everything you had on the court.

I came to anticipate his fiery talks and love them. He would challenge us and we would respond, time and again.

We had three or four assistant coaches. They were the therapists. They would show us support after we got yelled at by Coach Calhoun.

I never needed that kind of therapy. The yelling didn't upset me. It just made me more determined. Sometimes, though, I showed a look of anguish on my face when he was screaming because I knew that's what he was looking for and I didn't want him to feel he was wasting his breath.

After wins, Coach Calhoun let us enjoy the victory, but made sure we weren't too satisfied with ourselves. "Great job, fellas," he would say, patting several of us on our backs, "but let's continue to build on this."

After losses, it was, "What the hell bleep, bleep, bleep. We can do better, but I love you guys."

In film sessions with the whole team present, Coach Calhoun didn't hesitate to embarrass those of us who deserved it. He'd show me getting dunked on and say, "That's on you. You've got to bring it back right in his fucking face. I don't know what you were thinking."

He would pause the tape, let everybody laugh, then get on the rest of the team, saying, "Where's the help? Why's it late?"

He'd bring up the names of former players when he thought that would be effective. "Ray Allen wouldn't have let us lose that game," Coach Calhoun would say. "He wouldn't have let that happen."

That was a direct shot at me.

So when I made a mistake, I knew I had to come up with a huge play, do something to offset the damage I had done, and make sure we won that game. If not, I would be held accountable, especially in my second season when I had become the leader of the team.

One mistake Coach Calhoun warned us about was overdoing our frustration over a bad call to the point where we would wind up with a technical foul, or even ejection. He told us that, in his entire career, he had never seen an official make a call, and then, because a player bitched and moaned, change that call. Once the call is made, he said, it's over. Deal with it.

In addition to Coach Calhoun, we had the benefit of some unofficial coaches. Former Huskies like Ray Allen, Richard Hamilton, and Donyell Marshall, guys who knew what it was like to play in the NBA, were always coming back to the campus and schooling us on game preparation and fundamentals. Thanks to them, when I got to the NBA, I was ready to play at that level.

As the season went along, I learned to love going to the big-city arenas in New York and Boston. The atmosphere in Madison Square Garden when facing St. John's was awesome. If you couldn't get inspired playing in that environment, then you didn't belong on the court.

I particularly enjoyed the loud and rowdy crowds. Some fans on the road who knew my background would, during my pregame introduction, yell, "C-O-N-N-V-I-I-C-T. C-O-N-N-V-I-I-C-T." I'd laugh and respond with, "I'm going to shut all your asses up in about two minutes."

There was nothing as enjoyable as quieting an opposing crowd.

But it was also very enjoyable to have a friendly crowd sitting right on top of us at UConn home games.

The weirdest moment of my first season occurred in a game against Boston College at the Hartford Civic Center.

Although my mom did her best to make child support payments to Danisha for Camary, she had fallen behind. As a result, I got served papers at that game. As I was trotting off the court, this guy came running up to me and said, "Caron Butler?"

Seeing the man was holding a piece of paper and assuming he wanted me to put an autograph on it, I stopped and said, "Hey, how are you doing?"

Instead of handing me a pen, he gave me the piece of paper and said, "Here, take this with you."

I looked at it and did a double take. It was a claim for child support in arrears.

"Oh shit," I thought and tried to give it back to him.

"Nope," the guy said, "you've been served."

Then he was gone, leaving me standing on the court, wondering, "How did he get me?"

We finished the 2000–2001 season with a 20-12 record, not bad for a lot of teams, but frustrating for us. Because with just an 8-8 record in the Big East, a loss to Syracuse in the Big East tournament, and a miserable 1-8 record on the road, we didn't even make the NCAA tournament. We were the defending national champions, but we weren't going to be able to defend our title.

Instead, we had to settle for the NIT.

We beat South Carolina 72–65 in the first round, but lost to the University of Detroit Mercy 67–61 in the next round.

Extremely disappointed by the unexpected outcome of my first season at the Division I level, I decided to turn in my uniform and go pro. Having averaged 16 points a game, I figured I could be a late first-round pick or at least a second-rounder in the draft.

"I'm going to the NBA," I told Coach Calhoun.

"No, you're not," he said.

"Man, I'm leaving," I insisted.

"Nope," he told me. "You are going to get stronger. You are going to get better. And next year, you are going to have an even better opportunity because you know what to expect now. You know what to do."

I listened to Coach Calhoun. I knew he had my back.

At the end of my first school year, with my basketball and training schedule considerably lighter, I wanted to spend my extra free time with Andrea. I suggested we have a movie night in our dorm. She said she'd take care of the flick and I was in charge of the snacks.

She still kids me about my choice of refreshments for that night: Ding Dongs and chips. Guess Andrea expected something with more nutritional value from a workout fiend/gym rat who was never out of shape.

I can't fault her for her movie choice: *Love & Basketball*, my two favorite subjects. During the film, I leaned over to Andrea, who then wore glasses, and asked her to take them off.

"For what?" she said. "I can't see without them."

She told me to sit down and watch the movie and that was that.

School ended shortly afterward and Andrea took off for New Haven. We didn't even exchange phone numbers.

I grew a lot that summer in terms of experience and maturity on the court. I made the USA Basketball team, coached by Jim Boeheim, whose Syracuse squad had eliminated us from the Big East tournament. All but one of my teammates on that USA squad went on to play in the NBA, including Carlos Boozer, Jason Kapono, Jameer Nelson, Nick Collison, Brian Cook, Troy Bell, and Chris Duhon. We played in the World Championship for Young Men (those aged twenty-one and under) in Saitama, Japan, went undefeated, and won the gold medal, beating Croatia 89–80 in the title-winning game.

It was the culmination of a wonderful experience for me. My time with Boeheim was short, but he affected my career with one talk when he told me in practice one day halfway through the tournament that I was being too passive on offense, that with the combination of my size and mobility, I could be a dominant player if only I would take advantage of the skill set I had been blessed with.

Facing Israel in our next game, I finally unleashed my own game, responding to Boeheim's advice by scoring 21 points in a 98–74 victory, my highest point total of the tournament.

In the gold medal game against Croatia, I played 35 minutes, getting 15 points (6 for 9 from the floor), 4 rebounds, and 3 steals.

I was on a team with elite players and I performed at an elite level. Coach Calhoun had been right. I wasn't quite ready for the NBA after one season at UConn. But being on the USA Basketball squad, competing at the international level, attracting NBA scouts who flocked to those games, and then coming back to UConn for another season enabled me to hone my skills and increase awareness of me around the NBA, raising my stock enough to make me a high first-round pick.

I'm so glad I stayed at UConn for my sophomore year.

There was another big reason I was glad I stayed.

Andrea later told me that she heard on the news that my team had won the gold and thought to herself, "I wonder if he remembers me."

There was no chance I'd forget. I may not have known where my future lay in basketball at that point, but I had no doubt about my future with Andrea.

Our relationship didn't start in earnest until our sophomore year. Our first date was at Uno Pizzeria in November of 2001. We talked and talked that night. I told Andrea about my family and my past, about my dreams of playing in the NBA, how I was anxious to enter the draft and how agents were starting to stalk me in order to sign me and all the chaos that created.

For most of what I was telling her, I might as well have spoken in a foreign language. Andrea knew nothing about the behind-the-scenes wheeling and dealing of agents and the machinations of the draft.

Her family didn't follow basketball too closely until she brought me home. But once everybody learned the game and started following me as I entered the NBA, Andrea's mother, Shirley, became one of my most devoted fans. But she found that, when I was in a close game, she got so nervous that she couldn't watch.

Even to this day, if the score of my game is close going into the final minutes, Shirley will get up from the TV, go into the kitchen, and pretend to cook or do the dishes, but will yell out every few minutes, "What's going on?"

As the months went by and Andrea and I became closer and closer, spending more and more time with each other, I realized I was in love with her and wanted to share my life with her.

We loved going to the movies, and one night in February of 2002, we were in a theater at a concession stand getting our refreshments before seeing *Collateral Damage*, starring Arnold Schwarzenegger.

I looked at the ring Andrea wore on her left hand and said, "Oh, that's nice. Where did you get it?"

"It's a birthstone ring my grandmother gave me," she said. "My birthstone is a pearl."

"Can I see it?" I asked.

Andrea pulled the ring off her finger and handed it to me. Just then, the server returned with our snacks, distracting her, so she momentarily forgot about the ring, which I quickly slipped into my pocket.

We went into the show, the lights went out, *Collateral Damage* began, and she became engrossed in the movie. I then pulled out another ring, an engagement ring I had bought at J. B. Robinson Jewelers, using Pell Grant money.

"Oh, here's your ring back," I whispered.

Andrea didn't take her eyes off the screen as I slipped my ring onto her finger in the dark.

It didn't take long for her to realize the object on her finger was bigger and heavier than the one she had been wearing.

"What is this???" she said, her voice rising well above a whisper. "It isn't *my* ring."

Through the light from the flickering screen, Andrea could see that it was an engagement ring.

"Will you marry me?" I asked.

"Yes!!" she screamed, drowning out the actors on the screen.

"Calm down," I told her. "We'll talk after the show."

So we actually finished watching the movie, although we barely paid attention to it, Arnold's menacing presence fading far into the background in our minds.

Andrea later told me that she was in shock. At nineteen, she was two years younger than me. She wondered what her mother's reaction would be to our engagement. Andrea had been five when her mother and father separated, and she had lived in an all-female household ever since. She had never brought a guy home, never even used the word "boyfriend."

By the time we got out of the theater, however, Andrea's euphoria, matching mine, had swept her doubts away. I felt like I had just sunk a basket to win the NCAA tournament or the NBA title, while she proudly shared her joy on the phone with her mother, then her grandmother, then her sister, then everybody else she knew.

The joy turned to sadness a week later when Andrea's grandmother, Myrtle, had a heart attack.

Fortunately, Andrea was home visiting when her grandmother called from work to complain of chest pains. Knowing how stubborn her grandmother could be, Andrea figured she would just stay at work, hoping to ride the pain out.

So, Andrea raced over there, picked her grandmother up, and took her to a nearby hospital. When the wait to see a doctor took excruciatingly long, Andrea, acting with admirable urgency, helped her grandmother back into the car and drove over to Yale–New Haven Hospital. Andrea knew they would get better service there because her sister worked there.

When the heart attack was discovered and surgery was immediately scheduled, the whole family quickly gathered at the hospital.

I soon joined them. It was the first time I met her grandmother, her mother, her sister, and the rest of her family. Her grandmother was in a hospital bed in the hallway about to be wheeled into surgery when I came along.

She motioned for me to come over. As I bent down, she said softly, "I know all about you and I love you. If something happens to me, take care of my granddaughter, my baby, for me."

An angioplasty was performed on her grandmother, but when her condition failed to improve, the doctors went back in and performed a triple bypass. She finally came out of surgery three to four hours later with all her vital signs within acceptable range.

While I had gotten to know Andrea's family, she found out about one member of my family by accident.

A car accident.

My daughter, Camary, was hit by a vehicle back in Racine, and there was a little story about it in the UConn campus newspaper.

When Andrea saw it, she called and said, "Caron, you have a daughter?"

I told her I did and that I was on my way home to see how Camary was.

Fortunately, she was fine.

And so too was Andrea when she found out I also had a son. She accepted everything that had happened in my past, loving me for who I was—making me happier than ever that I gave her that ring.

Training for my second season at UConn began right after I got back from Japan, but I enthusiastically suited up because I felt I was better prepared than I had ever been for a new season.

Right from the start, we all felt it was going to be a very different season than the last one. And it was.

We won our first three games and six of our first seven.

A year earlier, we finished 20-12. This time, we wound up 27-7.

A year earlier, we were 8-8 in the Big East. This time, we were 13-3.

A year earlier, we were 1-8 on the road. This time, we were 7-3.

A year earlier, we were knocked out of the Big East tournament in one game. This time, we beat Villanova, Notre Dame, and Pittsburgh to become Big East champions and I was named MVP of the tournament. I was also co-Big East Player of the Year.

A year earlier, we finished the season in the NIT. This time, we made it to the NCAA tournament.

Going to that tournament for the first time was an amazing experience for me.

As we headed down the streets of Washington, DC, in our team bus, complete with a police escort, for our opening game at MCI Center against Hampton University, Coach Calhoun motioned for me to come up and sit next to him in the front.

He seemed like a man at peace with himself in the midst of this pressure cooker, and he tried to pass that feeling on to me.

"Son, remember this moment," he told me. "This is basketball at its purest. In the next phase of your career, the pros, there will be politics, but right now, it's pure. So enjoy it."

I didn't really understand what he meant at that moment. I had too many thoughts of excitement, anxiety, anticipation, and uncertainty running through my head. I was a player torn between confidence and concern. But now after thirteen seasons in the NBA, I can understand what he meant and appreciate what I had at that moment. That conversation with Coach Calhoun has stuck with me through my whole career.

In that tournament run, I learned a lot about myself. I learned I could perform at an extremely high level. Having prepared for that spotlight all my life, I told myself not to analyze the situation too much, but to just go off my instincts and play hard, and it worked.

I learned about winning. I didn't question my judgment on the court or second guess my decisions. Instead, I kept my focus on the next play, the next game, the next victory.

And I learned that I had leadership qualities. When we were down in the tournament, as every team is at some point, I was able to keep my poise and say the right things to my teammates at the right moment. I would always seem to come up with exactly the words that needed to be said.

In speaking up in the locker room, I made sure my teammates understood that I wasn't trying to talk down to them, but as one of them.

I would say things like, "Look, I'm not exempt, I fucked up, too. I should not have gone for that reach and gotten a foul. But look, it's a four-point game and we can win this shit."

In my first season, it was always Coach Calhoun speaking to us. But in my second year, I took more ownership in the team. He didn't always have to yell. I knew when he was mad because I was equally mad. So I jumped in before he could unleash one of his "What the bleep, bleep, bleep . . ." tirades. I would tell my teammates, "Either you are going to listen to me or you are going to have to listen to Coach and that might fuck up your whole day."

We were very close as a team that season. We all had rooms together on one floor of a dorm, so I saw my teammates every day. I saw them more than I saw my own family. In a way, at that point in my life, they were my family.

We didn't need players-only meetings like they sometimes have in the NBA with the coach asked to leave the room, because we talked all the time off the court and aired out any issues before they became problems.

Our success at the end of that season took us deep into the NCAA tournament. After beating Hampton 78–67 in our first-round game, we defeated North Carolina State 77–74 and Southern Illinois 71–59 to put us in the Elite Eight. We were in the East Regional finals against Maryland in the Carrier Dome in Syracuse.

The Terrapins had had a great season, coming into our game with a 29-4 record. We were coming in with a twelve-game winning streak. I felt this was the championship game right here. Whoever won would go on to win the NCAA title. And I was right. Unfortunately, I was wrong about who was going to win that game.

Getting two early fouls, I played only 13 minutes in the first half and scored just 6 points. I admit I was playing too aggressively because, in a game like that, every possession was crucial. One of the two fouls I picked up was a cheap one. There were two of us around the play and the official pointed to me. It could have gone against either of us. Coach Calhoun had a rule that any player who gets two fouls in the first half has to sit out until halftime. He wasn't willing to take the risk of breaking that rule on my behalf. Especially since the game was close and we wound up only seven points back at the half.

As I sat there on the bench, watching the minutes tick away in that first half, I was wondering if this was the moment that was going to define my collegiate career. I knew that, if we lost, it was probably going to be my last game, because I had all but made up my mind to go pro at season's end.

There were family and friends in the crowd who had driven all the way up from Racine to support me, and I felt like I had let them down.

But at halftime, I snapped out of my funk. "Fuck this," I told my teammates. "They are going to have to drag me off the court. I gotcha all this next half. I gotcha all. Just follow my lead."

Everybody was fired up.

I didn't even warm up and take any shots prior to the start of the second half. "I'm ready already," I told Coach Calhoun.

I knew what I was capable of. In our victory over North Carolina State two games earlier, I had scored a career-high 34 points.

As I walked onto the court, I looked back at all the coaches and said, "Watch this."

I hit my first jumper, my first three three-point attempts, and went on to score 26 points in the second half, 32 for the game. I was so emotional on the court at the thought of never putting my UConn uniform on again.

It was a tight game all the way down the stretch, neither team leading by more than three points from the 14-minute mark of the second half until just 36 seconds remained in the game.

The dagger to our hopes was a three-point basket by Steve Blake with 25 seconds remaining and the shot clock running down. He had missed his two other shot attempts, but this one gave the Terrapins an 86–80 lead in a game they would win 90–82.

As both Coach Calhoun and I had predicted, the winner went on to the NCAA title. Maryland beat Kansas to advance to the championship game, then defeated Indiana 64–52 in the finale.

For me, when our game was over, I knew that was it. I think everybody in the locker room knew it as well because I was so quiet. Normally, even after a loss, I would come in, give everybody around the room a high five, and have something positive to say about the future.

But this time, for me, there was no future at UConn. I just sat there with my head down, trying to gather my thoughts.

On the bus ride out of the Carrier Dome, Coach Calhoun again asked me to sit with him.

"It's time for you to go," he said, relieving me of the tension surrounding my decision. "You are going to be a lottery pick."

"You think so?" I said.

"I know so," he replied. Coach Calhoun always had a good sense of what was going on with NBA teams. "We are going to have the press conference in two days."

I should have been used to moving on. I had survived leaving Racine and survived leaving MCI, but leaving UConn was even tougher. I knew I'd always go back to Racine, and MCI wasn't the same without Max. UConn had helped me grow so much as a person and as a basketball player. I had gotten accustomed to the UConn family and lifestyle. Leaving all that behind left me uncertain about the future. So it was really hard to say goodbye, though I knew nobody was going to feel sorry for me. I was living my dream, heading for the NBA. I was just thinking how nice it would be to take, along with Andrea, the rest of my UConn family with me.

I feel like I took a piece of UConn with me, and I left a piece of myself that will always be there.

FIFTEEN

MY YEARS IN THE NBA: RILES, KOBE, K.D., AND GUNPLAY IN THE LOCKER ROOM

MIAMI HEAT

After all the physical preparation prior to the draft, the mental agony of hearing name after name called in the first round without so much as a phone call to let me know I had not been forgotten, and the ultimate elation when the Heat finally informed me they would picking me at No. 10, I figured it would be chill time.

After the lights and cameras were turned off and the reporters had left with their tape recorders and notebooks full, there would be plenty of time to kick back, right?

I could spend much of the first two months of summer working out, packing up my belongings, looking for a place to live in Miami, and getting familiar with the town.

How dumb was I?

My leisurely summer didn't even last long enough for me to get off the podium after posing for pictures with Commissioner Stern.

Right then, my phone rang. It was Pat Riley, Miami coach and team president.

"Hey, I'm so happy you are with the Heat," he said. "You ready to work?"

"Yes," I replied.

"Alright, a plane will be there tomorrow morning to pick you up."

"Man, I got to find a place to stay," I said.

"Yeah, find a place," Riley replied. "Get settled. But you are going to be here."

"So I don't get to go home?"

"Nope, it's business time."

So much for my summer vacation.

As I flew south with all sorts of decisions to make concerning my new life in a new city, it was comforting to know that the financial side of turning pro was not going to be a distraction, because I had Raymond Brothers as my agent. And he had my back.

Raymond was recommended to me by a UConn coach who told me, "He's a genuine dude who is all about the athlete and will work his tail off for you."

By the time I met Raymond, I had already talked to five other agents. I found that most of them, in speaking to athletes, especially younger athletes, didn't want to discuss the percentage that they charge. They just say things like, "You are going to be the next Kobe. What do you want, a truck?"

I told one agent, "If I'm going to be a millionaire, I can buy my own truck. Correct me if I'm wrong, but nine times out of ten, that truck would not be coming out of your pocket. It would be coming out of mine. And you are going to find a way to pay yourself twice."

Needless to say, I didn't hire that agent.

When Raymond and I got together, he told me, "I would go to bat for you. I don't have a lot of clients, but I fight for the ones I do represent."

I really liked his energy. So much so, that, rather than requiring a second or third meeting, or going through a prolonged vetting process, or asking for references, I looked him in the eye and said, "I want you to be my agent, man."

"Really?" said Raymond, getting a decision far quicker than he had expected.

"Yes," I told him, "I like what you are saying. I like the way you present yourself, carry yourself. I want you to be my agent."

I picked him right there on the spot and Raymond has been my agent ever since.

Right after the press conference I held to announce that I was leaving UConn, Raymond asked me what I needed. I told him there were only three things on my to-do list: I wanted my mom to be immediately put on an allowance because I was already negotiating a deal with Nike and the numbers they were talking about were in the millions. I needed to take Andrea with me to L.A., where I had decided I would train prior to the draft. And I needed to buy a car.

"That's it," I told Raymond. "I don't need anything else."

The toughest of my three requests, as it turned out, was getting Andrea on board.

She didn't need convincing, but her mother did. Myrtle was not going to let her nineteen-year-old daughter take off with a basketball player rather than stay in school. Her mother placed a high premium on education and, not knowing anything about the NBA, wasn't convinced I could count on basketball as a career. A degree seemed a lot safer.

So even though we were engaged, Andrea's mother told her, "No, you are not going across the country with some guy."

Further complicating the situation, Kasia, her sister, was graduating from the University of Hartford on the day I was scheduled to fly to L.A.

Torn between me and her mother, Andrea cried for two days. While she loved me, she was not going to disrespect her mother and leave without her blessing.

Finally, seeing how much it meant to Andrea, her mother said, "Go."

But while Andrea may have gotten her way about coming to L.A., her mom was determined to see that her daughter came back to finish her education. So, before departing, Andrea had to leave a deposit for a room at UConn for the following semester.

Andrea didn't forget her sister. She attended Kasia's graduation, saw her walk up to the stage to get her diploma, then raced to the airport to meet me for the flight to L.A.

Why Los Angeles? I wanted to be away from everybody in order to have peace of mind and stay focused. I didn't know anybody out in L.A., and nobody knew me because I had been playing on the East Coast. It'd be perfect.

Once out there, I got the car I wanted, an SUV that I was going to give to my mother when I came back to Racine. Instead, it was stolen while we were still in L.A.

But it all turned out fine. I had Andrea with me, I got another car, I got in my training, I got selected in the first round, and I got on the private jet sent by Riley (Riles as we all referred to him), accompanied to my new home by Andrea, her mom, my mom, my brother, Junior, and Raymond.

I had one bit of unfinished business to deal with before joining the Heat. There were three major drug dealers formerly from the Racine area—Michael, Dennis, and Clifford—who had helped me out financially at times when I still lived there.

Detective Rick Geller and other Racine law enforcement officials had put so much heat on the three of them that they had relocated to Minnesota. But as far as Rick was concerned, that wasn't far enough away to get them out of my life now that I was entering the pro spotlight. So after the draft, Rick sent me a letter to say, "Ultimately, this is your decision, but if I were you, I would write each of those three a check, tell them, 'Good luck in life,' and be done with it. Don't even have their names associated with you."

That's exactly what I did, telling them, "Thanks a lot for helping me out when I needed it, and here's a little bit of a thank-you."

When I reached Miami, I hit the ground running.

Literally.

There were workouts, there was the summer league, there were obligations to fulfill with Nike once I signed a contract with them, and before I knew it, it was time for training camp leading into the season.

People warned me about hitting the rookie wall halfway through the season. That was understandable. An NBA team's forty-first game in an eighty-two-game regular season is already more than an entire college season. And that's not even counting the playoffs.

I thought I had hit the rookie wall halfway through training camp because we ran so much. That first Heat camp was the toughest one of my basketball career. Riles totally wore out my ass, nearly killed me. It was the hardest anybody had ever worked me: body, mind, and soul.

I was losing weight and that can be good in training camp, but not when you lose as much as I did.

I had only been in camp for two weeks when I woke up burning hot early one morning. I stumbled out of bed, walked into the bathroom where the tile on the floor was cold, took off my shorts and shirt, and lay down naked.

It may have been a cold surface, but I was still boiling. What the hell was going on with me? Andrea heard me and came in to see if I was okay.

Far from it.

She took me to a nearby hospital where they determined I was severely dehydrated and running a high temperature. They gave me an IV, put me on ice, and kept me in bed for three days.

Riles called. He just wanted to let me know I was missing practice.

By the time I left the hospital, I had lost twenty pounds. I headed right back to practice, but I was too embarrassed to tell anyone what had happened, so I said I had caught the flu.

Drink more water, I was told. It's not the practices that can fry you, but the lack of fluids in your body.

Rookie mistake No. 1.

I was extremely athletic and had good size. But when I arrived from UConn, I did need to lose a little weight—though certainly not as much as I did—and get into shape for the marathon season ahead.

Once I figured out the routine, took my water breaks, and got with the program, Riles and his staff whipped me into supreme condition. I got more explosive and was ready to take on the challenge of the transition to the next level.

I will never forget my first NBA game. It was the season opener in Miami against the Orlando Magic. I was so excited. I had so much I wanted to show the basketball world. The anticipation left such a tight knot in my stomach that I felt like I was going to explode. This was the opportunity of a lifetime.

My first basket came off a missed shot by teammate Malik Allen (funny, he became one of my coaches later with the Detroit Pistons). When the ball bounced off the glass, I went up and slammed it down through the hoop with a tomahawk dunk, the first 2 of 16 points I scored that night along with 7 rebounds and 3 assists in 34 minutes.

I'll admit it. I was trying to make a name for myself, and it all begins with the first impression. That first game was definitely a great way to start.

But I quickly got over the surreal experience of being in an NBA game and understood that it wasn't about me. It was about the team. I learned so much playing under the great Pat Riley and the members of his staff back then such as Stan Van Gundy, Erik Spoelstra, and Keith Askins, while playing alongside veterans like Eddie Jones and Brian Grant.

I also have to give a special shout-out to Alonzo Mourning. Although he sat out my rookie season because of a kidney disease that resulted in a transplant, he was always around that year, taking the time to share his wisdom and offering words of encouragement despite what he was going through. That showed me a lot.

I've been able to maintain my game all these years because of what those Heat veterans and coaches instilled in me at an early age. Their insight and advice didn't fall on deaf ears. And as of this writing, I'm preaching what I learned to the younger guys I play with on the Pistons.

The goals are simple and basic. In order to have longevity in this league, you have to buy in to the established standards of whatever team you are on, become part of something larger than yourself, and stay with the program in good times and bad. You've got to be honest with yourself at all times and police yourself when necessary. And you've always got to be accountable.

As a rookie, I had so much to learn. In the beginning, I didn't even know how to get to the airport in Miami. At first, with no GPS back then, I had to trail a teammate's car to get there.

I hadn't planned on trailing my teammates when it came to after-hours adventures.

"Hey, rook," they'd say, "you've got to come out."

"I don't want to go out," I insisted. "I'm on a budget. I don't want to spend a lot of money."

"No, you've got to come. We are going to introduce you to NBA nightlife."

So I went. It was eye-opening to see my teammates throwing $6,000 to $7,000 in small bills up toward the ceiling in various clubs and watching people scramble to pick them up.

I just couldn't do that after what I had been through in my life and what I had seen my mom and grandmother go through to eke out a living. I enjoyed being with those players, but I couldn't buy into that lifestyle. I have too much respect for my past and for the grind so many people have to go through to survive. Being a witness to that humbled me, and I have tried to stay that way throughout my career.

Everything was different on the inside than it was when I had been on the outside looking in. When you are a fan and your team plays back-to-back games, you're happy. You get to watch them two nights in a row. But when you're a member of the team, you realize back-to-back means playing a game, usually heading straight to the airport, hopping on a plane, flying to another city, maybe getting in at 3:00 or 4:00 in the morning, catching a few hours of sleep, going to a shootaround, and then, a few hours later, playing another game.

In college, we only played back-to-back games in tournaments, and those games were played at the same location. The NBA pace never slowed down until the season ended.

In my first two years, I was in awe whenever I looked around the court and saw the players I was facing, people I'd only seen on TV like MJ, Kobe, Tracy McGrady, Vince Carter, and Paul Pierce. I learned how hard these big names worked away from public view to earn the stardom fans bestowed upon them. We would come to the Indianapolis arena that was then known as Conseco Fieldhouse more than two hours before our tipoff against the Pacers and find that Reggie Miller had been there two hours before that, shooting, shooting, shooting. I could hear the ball bouncing while I was walking through the tunnel.

I had heard the stories and myths about NBA players, but now they were people who had become part of my daily life. I'd go to a boxing match and find myself sitting next to Magic Johnson. I thought, "Man, I'm really living this life."

One of the highlights of my career occurred in Miami against Michael Jordan, who was then playing the final games of his career for the Washington Wizards.

Prior to the tipoff, the Heat, in a ceremony officiated by Riles, honored Jordan, who would retire at the end of the season. After the game, he walked to half court and shook Riles's hand.

Spotting me watching from the sideline, MJ yelled out, "Young fellow!" and motioned for me to come over. When I did, he said, "Hey man, you're going to be a great player. Keep up the good work." Then he gave me a hug.

I walked away thinking, "Damn, that was Michael Jordan telling me I'm going to be a great player." I can't describe how good that felt, what a boost it gave to my confidence level.

We didn't come close to making the playoffs in my rookie year, finishing the season last in the Atlantic Division at 25-57.

A frustrated Riles told me, "We've got to go a little harder next season so we've got to get you really ready."

This time, I was going to bring my water bottle with me.

I took a week off and then was right back at it.

During the offseason, my teammates were going to places like Cancun, St. Thomas, and all sorts of other exotic destinations I hadn't heard of. It was a whole new world for me. My idea of a vacation was going into my mom's backyard in Racine and putting my feet up. If I really wanted to get away, I'd go to Chicago.

As I returned for my second season with the Heat, I was blindsided by a stunning announcement. Riles's parting comment to me at the end of my rookie season left me dreading just how tough the upcoming training camp might be. But as I learned that day, I was about to face something even more alarming for a young player with much still to learn, a training camp without Riles.

As my teammates and I came into the locker room after a practice on October 24, 2003, Riles asked us all to sit down.

He seemed very focused, very serious.

"I'm going to tell you all a story," Riles said, "a story that best illustrates transition in this league. It's a story about Kareem Abdul-Jabbar, who I had the honor of coaching for many seasons with the Lakers.

"Toward the end of his career, when he was in his early forties, he had a horrible game. With just he and I in the locker room, I pulled up a chair for him, set up a projector, and had him watch a tape of himself in that game, a tape of the mistakes and poor plays he had made. I wanted him to deal with the harsh truth, with the fact that he couldn't perform at a high level anymore. He had to accept that."

I wasn't sure where Riles was going with this, but he soon got to the point, a painful point for both him and our team.

"Every one of you will have a moment like that," he said, "when you will have to make a transition in your life as will every one in every other profession. You will have to leave something behind that you love, but can no longer do. I never fully appreciated the magnitude of that moment for Kareem, sitting there watching that tape, facing his reality, until now when I'm sitting here facing my reality.

"Today, I'm walking away from this job. I'll still be here as the team president, but I will no longer be the coach. It's time to have new blood in here. Stan Van Gundy will be your new coach."

There was dead silence when Riles was done. None of us knew what to say.

He stood up, walked out of the locker room, went upstairs to the waiting media, and told the world what he had just told us.

As I got older, I understood the depth of his remarks. I learned a lot from Riles. He used to write personal messages to each of us, usually selecting players who had had a bad game. We called them "the blue papers," because that was the color he chose.

At first, I hated getting them. He would go on and on about the history of the Lakers, and what Magic did, and how hard and long the Showtime teams worked in the gym. He'd sum up the letter with a thought like, "This is the circle of life. This is what it's all about."

On the road, Riles would slide the blue papers under the door of our hotel rooms. So every trip, if I had a bad game, I knew there would be blue under my door.

As time went on, I looked forward to reading the blue papers. They always kept me engaged and motivated.

I needed all the encouragement I could get at the start of my second season in Miami after suffering a knee injury that required arthroscopic surgery just a week before the start of the season. I missed the first six games.

A doctor told Raymond, "You need to tell that kid that he might not be able to play again."

Fortunately, Raymond wasn't so quick to give up.

"I am not going to tell that kid any such thing," he said. "We will follow God's plan and see what happens."

Raymond didn't tell me any of this until after the crisis had passed. And it did pass. I came back too soon, averaging 4.3 points in my first eight games. So I sat out another seven, working hard on my rehab. It was seventeen games before I scored in double figures for the first time. And it was a little over two months after the surgery before I was back to my normal self on the court.

My ability to bounce back was matched by the team's comeback from the previous season. Even though we finished only two games above .500 at 42-40, we wound up second in the Atlantic Division, earning us a berth in the playoffs.

In my first postseason series, we faced the then–New Orleans Hornets. They took us the distance, but we won Game 7 by the score of 85–77. I was fortunate enough to lead the team in scoring in that game with 23 points and tied for the team high in rebounds with 9. But we lost in the next round, the conference semifinals, to the Indiana Pacers in six games.

I was left with a good feeling about myself and the team. My future in Miami seemed assured, but I had a lot to learn about the business of the NBA, and I was about to get a lesson that would rattle my life.

Los Angeles Lakers

During the offseason, Andrea and I went to the West Indies island of Antigua with Erik Spoelstra, representing the Heat and the NBA at a Read to Achieve event. We held a basketball clinic with the local kids, read books with them, and were there for the opening of a new library.

On the return trip, I started hearing rumblings that Shaquille O'Neal was about to be traded by the Lakers and Miami was a possible destination.

At first I was excited. Shaq wanted to play with us? Yes! We were a rising power and this would only make us better. Much better.

The question was, who would have to go to make this happen? I was shocked to hear my own name mentioned along with Lamar Odom, the feeling being that the Lakers wanted young talent in exchange and the swap made sense salarywise.

I asked Erik about the possibility that I'd be gone, and he assured me I was safe.

Two days later, we landed at Miami International Airport. When we got to baggage claim, Erik went his way and I went mine along with Andrea.

All of a sudden, a guy came up to me and said, "Thank you for everything. Good luck out there in L.A."

"What are you talking about?" I asked.

"Man, you are going to the Lakers. You are a Laker now."

I hadn't gotten a phone call or anything, and the news was already on SportsCenter.

Riles called me right after that and said, "Caron, you have to understand, it's Shaq."

I told him I totally got it. I lied. I really didn't, but at that moment, I didn't know what else to say.

Along with me, Riles traded Lamar, Brian Grant, and a future first-round pick (the Lakers used it for Jordan Farmar in 2006) for Shaq, then the most dominating center in the game.

I felt bad, helpless. I realized I didn't have any control over my career.

Raymond, my agent, told me, "That's part of the business, young fella, but we are going to be alright. Hey, you get a chance to go to L.A. and play with Kobe."

I was looking forward to that. But it was still tough to leave Dwyane Wade and all the other people in an organization that had helped me so much. Those are relationships that last long after basketball.

The guys I played with were hurt by the trade, but no one more so than Dwyane. He came to my house and told me, "I can't believe this shit. Call Riles and tell him, no. Tell him you don't want to go to L.A."

"I don't have any control over it," I said. "I'm gone."

In response to my departure, Dwyane did something that deeply touched me, something I'll never forget. He wrote my initials on his game shoes, announcing to the basketball world how he felt about the trade. In response, I put his initials on my shoes. We were like brothers.

I respected Riles when I played for him, but that respect went to an even higher level after he traded me, even though I wasn't happy with him at that moment, Shaq or no Shaq.

Riles continued to send me letters, those blue papers, once a month for more than a year after I left. He cared enough about me to stay in my life even though I was no longer one of his players, no longer contributing to the Heat. That's class.

I have maintained a special connection with him through the years and his words, always putting life into proper perspective, have stayed with me.

When Lamar, Brian, and I arrived in L.A., Lakers general manager Mitch Kupchak told us to reach out to Kobe.

When I got him on the phone, Kobe used almost the same words Riles had said to me two years earlier in our first conversation. For both, it boiled down to: *Great to have you, time to go to work.*

The Lakers had not renewed Coach Phil Jackson's contract, deciding instead to hire Rudy Tomjanovich. But after having my conversation with Kobe, I felt like *he* was the coach. And that was fine with me. Who wouldn't want to learn from the best?

I thought Riles was the toughest taskmaster I had ever trained under until I got introduced to Kobe workouts. He goes so hard and so long in the gym that he sometimes blacks out.

Any success I've had in my career began with what I learned from people like Kobe. He taught me so much about preparation, always maintaining the proper frame of mind, rechanneling my energy to get ready for the next challenge, going as hard as I could for as long as I could, staying goal oriented, and playing with an edge all the time. Being around him on the court and in the locker room, I learned something new every day.

He is misunderstood sometimes because people just see the relentless competitor. "You don't have time to befriend many people when you are grinding," Kobe once explained to me, "because you are too focused on trying to achieve goals."

But behind the clenched teeth and the take-no-prisoners stare, there is a good dude, a really good dude.

I got a memorable look at that dude on a Lakers trip to Milwaukee for a game against the Bucks.

Sitting on the bus for the ride into town, I couldn't wait to get some home cooking at my mother's house in Racine, thirty miles south. When I mentioned where I was headed, somebody said, "You inviting us over to eat?"

Great idea. I yelled that everybody on the team was welcome. Brian Grant said he'd come as did Lamar, Sasha Vujacic, Chris Mihm, and several others along with a couple of members of the training staff.

When I asked Kobe if he'd come, he said, "No doubt."

"You serious?" I asked. "Because if I tell my mother Kobe Bryant is coming for dinner, the whole family is going to go crazy."

He was serious.

I ordered a couple of SUVs, and Kobe and his security people piled in with everybody else.

When we got to my mom's house, there were almost fifty family members and friends there, many of them coming just to see if Kobe was really going to show up.

During dinner, as he ate some ribs, someone hanging over him, awed by being in his presence, said, "Kobe Bryant eats ribs?"

Kobe looked up, smiled, and said, "I pump gas, too."

When Kobe Bryant set foot in our house, it was a special moment for me and my family because I have so much respect for him as a player and as a person.

The Lakers asked me to go on the Jay Leno show. I was a little uncomfortable with the idea, because I had never been on a talk show like that and had certainly never opened up about the struggles in my life in front of a national audience. Nevertheless, I agreed to go, accompanied by John Black, Laker PR vice president.

It's a funny show and Jay is a funny guy. Backstage, I could hear him laughing and cracking jokes with the guests who were on before me. I wasn't laughing, because I was too busy thinking about what I would say. Hell, I didn't know any jokes.

When I came on stage, I was greeted with applause and cheers from the audience. That relaxed me a little. During the break that immediately followed, Jay leaned over to me as I got comfortable on the couch and said, "Don't worry, it's improv. We will just flow off each other. I'm going to ask you some stuff."

When the cameras went on, he innocently asked me some basic questions: where I was from and what had life been like for me as a child.

Audience members were still chuckling because they figured, with Jay running the show, there were more laughs ahead.

I started talking, and as the words came out and the memories were stirred, the tears started flowing. I quickly got into the painful parts of my early years in Racine, subjects I had never addressed publicly. Yet here I was dropping tears on *The Tonight Show*.

Jay seemed stunned. He didn't know what to say or do, so he just handed me a Kleenex and listened. It was as if he had injected me with truth serum, because I spilled my guts out. He wasn't expecting it. I know he wasn't because I wasn't.

Soon, we got back to lighter subjects. Jay asked me, if I could meet any Hollywood star at a game, who would it be?

I told him, "Halle Berry and Jennifer Fox."

After the show was over, as I was leaving, Jay told me, "Man, you've got a blockbuster story, a powerful testimony, and you should tell it. You should speak out more."

That's where I first got the idea for this book.

Halle must have seen the show because soon after, when she was asked in an interview on TNT who her favorite Laker was, she said, "I love Caron Butler."

I got a tape of that interview and kept it for years.

My chance to respond to her came one night at Staples Center when we were playing the Rockets. With Halle in a courtside seat, I decided that I was going to dunk on Yao Ming right in front of her. He blocked my first attempt, but I got a second chance coming down the baseline and boom, I got my dunk.

Had to put on a show for Halle.

WASHINGTON WIZARDS

After you get over the shock of leaving your first NBA team, it gets a lot easier to change uniforms when an opportunity presents itself. After one season with the Lakers, I took advantage of free agency to become a Wizard when they offered me a great deal.

Eddie Jordan, another former Laker, was the coach when I arrived. He was not only good at what he did, but he was a good person.

Of all the coaches I've had over the years, he was the only one who became a personal friend of mine off the court. I would go over to his house just to chill and talk to him.

On the court, he believed in me and my teammates, and put us in situations where we could prosper. He also taught us a lot of things beyond basketball. I love Eddie Jordan.

He was my coach in Washington for three full seasons and the first eleven games of my fourth year before he was fired after our team got off to a 1-10 start.

But he left me with something I will carry with me the rest of my life, my nickname. It was Eddie who came up with "Tuff Juice."

He started calling me that after hearing about the adversity I had been through in my life and watching me play through all sorts of injuries.

"You are one tough dude," Eddie said to me one day. He changed that to Tuff Juice, referring to the expression people use when someone is on a roll, saying, "You got the juice now."

The name just kind of stuck. I liked it, so I kept it.

Washington is where my career really took off. Over the four and a half seasons I was there, I averaged 18.9 points and 6.4 rebounds per game, shot 45.2 percent from the floor, and played in two All-Star Games.

My teammates in those years included Gilbert Arenas, Antawn Jamison, Brendan Haywood, and DeShawn Stevenson. We were young and so talented. Between Gilbert, Antawn, and me, we could score 72 points a night effortlessly, complementing each other in all aspects of the game.

But looking back, we really fucked up a good thing. We had the recipe, but we were childish. Add maturity, a more serious attitude, and a firm commitment to work together and who knows how far we could have gone. Instead, it was just one blown opportunity after another. In the years I was there, we got into the playoffs three times and were bumped out by the Cavaliers in the first round each time. That haunts me to this day. Damn, we could have been really good.

A chronic knee injury suffered by Gilbert that knocked him out of the playoffs altogether in 2006–2007 and before Game 5 in 2007–2008 didn't help either.

We were down three games to one to the Cavs in '08 with Game 5 in Cleveland. I was disappointed when Gilbert chose not to even go to support us.

Before we left, however, Abe Pollin, the Wizards owner, called us all into his office, the whole team (he had a big office), and told us, "I'm in a battle for my life because of a brain disorder. Out of some seven billion people in the world, this has happened to me. I don't know if we are going to win this series, but Game 5 can be our championship. If you guys go to Cleveland and win this game for me, it would mean so much."

I didn't say anything after the meeting, didn't even talk. I figured I would do my talking on the court in honor of Mr. Pollin.

And I did, going on to have one of my best playoff games. I had a team-high 32 points along with 9 rebounds and 5 assists, and I scored what would turn out to be the winning basket with LeBron James in my face, putting us on top with 3.9 seconds remaining.

LeBron tried to respond at the other end, but his shot at the buzzer missed, enabling us to hold on for an 88–87 victory.

I was so excited that I ran to the scorer's table and celebrated in front of the anguished fans. My joy was more for Mr. Pollin than for myself.

When we came back to Washington, he called me up to his office, gave me a hug, and told me how much he respected and loved me.

It was the only time Mr. Pollin ever talked to me about basketball in our many private conversations. Every other time he called me up, the only subject was family. He would ask, "How are your kids doing? Your mom? Your wife?" Even if we had a close game, he didn't want to talk about it. He wanted to talk about real life.

Unfortunately, we let him down the next day, losing Game 6 to the Cavs by a score of 105–88, eliminating us from the postseason once again. It would have been even more lopsided if we hadn't scored the last seven points of the game.

Mr. Pollin never saw his team in another playoff game, dying the following year at eighty-five. It has always bothered me that we didn't win that series for him.

There was one memorable moment in Wizards' history that I'm glad Mr. Pollin never saw. It occurred in December of 2009.

Gilbert, who had played a total of only fifteen regular-season games over the two previous seasons because of the chronic knee injury, had come back strong for 2009–2010, justifying the six-year, $111 million contract he had been given a year earlier. He had started all twenty-five of our games and was averaging 22 points, including 45 on December 18 against the Warriors.

On the flight home the next night after we lost at Phoenix, Gilbert, teammate Javaris Crittenton, and several other players were in a card game that got real heated. While Gilbert was a dominating presence on the team, Javaris didn't roll with some of his ways. The players were in seats facing each other with a pull-out table between them. I was in the seat next to them half asleep as we began our descent into DC.

My eyes popped open when I heard Javaris say, "Put the money back. Put the fucking money back."

"I ain't putting shit back," Gilbert replied. "Get it the way Tyson got the title. Might or fight or whatever you got to do to get your money back. Otherwise, you ain't gettin' it."

When Gilbert put the money in his pocket, Javaris lunged over the table to grab him. Antawn, seated across the aisle, leaped up, shoved Javaris's shoulder down on the table, and held it there with the full weight of his body while telling him to calm down.

I got up and yelled, "Hey, everybody shut the fuck up. How much was in the pot?"

It was $1,100.

"It shouldn't be that hard to pay what you owe him," I told Gilbert. "We all make a great living, so just pay the money."

A man who has a $111 million contract shouldn't be fighting over $1,100.

Message not received. The two of them kept arguing as we buckled up for the landing.

They were still going at it when we all got on an airport shuttle van to take us to our vehicles.

Ernie Grunfeld, the team president, leaned over to me and said in a pleading manner, "Talk to them."

"I did," I told him, "but they keep arguing."

Everyone could hear Gilbert and Javaris going at it as we rode along.

"I'll see your ass at practice and you know what I do," Gilbert said.

"What the fuck you mean, you know what I do?" replied Javaris.

"I play with guns."

"Well I play with guns, too."

We had the next day off, but on the following day, December 21, practice started at ten o'clock at the Verizon Center so we all wandered in a little earlier.

When I entered the locker room, I thought I had somehow been transported back to my days on the streets of Racine. Gilbert was standing in front of his two locker stalls, the ones previously used by Michael

Jordan, with four guns on display. Javaris was standing in front of his own stall, his back to Gilbert.

"Hey, MF, come pick one," Gilbert told Javaris while pointing to the weapons. "I'm going to shoot your ass with one of these."

"Oh no, you don't need to shoot me with one of those," said Javaris, turning around slowly like a gunslinger in the Old West. "I've got one right here."

He pulled out his own gun, already loaded, cocked it, and pointed it at Gilbert.

Other players who had been casually arriving, laughing and joking with each other, came to a sudden halt, their eyes bugging out. It took them only a few seconds to realize this was for real, a shootaround of a whole different nature. They all looked at each other and then they ran, the last man out locking the door behind him.

I didn't panic because I'd been through far worse, heard gunshots more times than I could count, and seen it all before. This would have been just another day on the south side.

I talked calmly to Javaris, reminding him that his entire career, not to mention, perhaps, his life, would be over if he flicked that trigger finger.

I looked back at Gilbert. He was silent as he removed himself from the scene.

Javaris slowly lowered the gun.

I know that Gilbert was thinking, "I went too far. I had a gun pointed at me and it was loaded."

Somebody outside the locker room called 911. Flip Saunders was the coach back then, but he was too scared to even come into the locker room.

In the months that followed, punishment was handed down by both the league and the courts. Gilbert and Javaris were each suspended for the final fifty games of the season. Gilbert pleaded guilty to one felony count of carrying a pistol without a license. He received two years of probation, thirty days in a halfway house, four hundred hours of community service, and was required to contribute $5,000 to a fund for crime victims.

Javaris pleaded guilty to a misdemeanor for unlawful possession of a firearm, got one year of probation, and had to pay a $1,250 fine and do community service.

His problems with the law, however, were just starting. In early 2015, Javaris pleaded guilty to murder and was sentenced to twenty-three years in prison.

I was under no illusions that many of the rest of us were not going to be affected by the gun incident. I knew this was the end of the Washington franchise as we had known it. With Mr. Pollin gone, a new regime coming in, and the image of the team shattered by guns that weren't even fired, it was time to tear up the Wizards, wipe the roster clean, and start all over again.

Grunfeld warned me that was going to happen. "We might have to trade everyone," he said. "Rebuild from scratch, looking forward to the future."

All I said was, "Okay." What else could I say?

While no one was shot in the Gilbert-Javaris confrontation, I wish I could say the same for a tragedy that occurred earlier in my Wizard days involving Black Rob, Robert Nellom, my closest friend from my days in the streets.

After getting out of jail, he went right back to a life of crime by staging a robbery. He went to a bar, locked the front door while customers were in there, made everybody undress, and took off with their wallets and purses, including money and identification cards.

The police were looking for Black Rob, but fortunately, I was able to get to him first because it was the offseason and I was in Racine.

When I found him, he admitted that he was the guilty party. He was lying low, going everywhere by bus instead of taking his car out on the streets where it might be spotted.

I told Black Rob to give me the wallets and purses and whatever money was left. I would make sure the robbery victims got their possessions back, putting in my own money to make up for anything he had already spent. I also gave him $3,000 to get him back on his feet.

"Man, I'm just trying to make this right," I said. "I'm in the NBA. I got money to smooth things over. I don't want you to go back to jail. You just got out."

Black Rob agreed to listen to me.

I contacted a friend of mine who was with the Racine Police Department. "Everybody got their money back," I told him, pleading Black Rob's case.

"He's got to come in," my friend said, "and undergo questioning, and then we'll try to help him."

I had to go back to DC, because I was promoting a concert and party with Lil Wayne. The last thing I told Black Rob was that they were expecting him to come in for questioning, but because the victims had been repaid, he would probably avoid more jail time. If there was a problem, call me.

There was a big problem. He chose not to talk to the cops.

Two days later, I got a phone call from an old Racine buddy. "Black Rob got shot three times, two in the chest, one in the head," I was told.

I started frantically calling Black Rob. Kept calling. Kept calling. No answer.

In the meantime, my phone was ringing like crazy, everybody in our old gang wanting to know if I had heard the news.

Finally came the call I had dreaded.

It was just two words: "He's dead."

I walked right out of the concert, hopped in my 600 Mercedes, and drove straight through from DC to Racine, a thirteen-hour trip.

I went right to the morgue where I found Black Rob's mother, his sister, and his brother.

When I saw Black Rob's body, the history of our lives together flashed before me.

I helped dress my friend and bury him. It was one of the hardest things I ever had to do in my entire life.

Black Rob was just twenty-three.

He was killed by a guy we knew growing up. Why did he kill Black Rob? I've never heard a good explanation. Black Rob's murderer is now in prison serving a life sentence.

Following the murders of James Barker Jr. and Dre (Andre King) during my teenage years, Black Rob's death completed a trilogy of death for me. It was a final act I never expected so many years later. But his passing was a jarring reminder that, even though I was far removed from my life on the streets, I was never more than a bullet away from being yanked back in.

And the Gilbert-Javaris incident showed me that if I thought an NBA locker room was a guaranteed safe haven from the world of guns and ammo I thought I had escaped from, I was fooling myself.

I had some great years in Washington, did well on the court, earned financial security, and met a lot of wonderful people.

But losing Black Rob, losing Mr. Pollin, and waiting for the tsunami about to envelop the Wizard roster after the suspensions of Gilbert and Javaris, I felt like I had a cloud of bad karma hanging over me.

My dreams of finally winning a championship hadn't faded, but I realized I would have to again change uniforms to change that karma and have a realistic chance of someday holding the Larry O'Brien Trophy.

DALLAS MAVERICKS

I will be forever grateful to Ernie Grunfeld. Given the task of tearing down the Wizards and rebuilding the team's image, Ernie negotiated a seven-player deal with the Mavericks that sent me to Dallas less than two months after Gilbert and Javaris had squared off in the locker room. Ernie put me in a situation where I could be successful with Mark Cuban, a great owner; Donnie Nelson, a smart general manager; Jason Kidd and other talented players; and a coach, Rick Carlisle, who is a basketball genius. Yes he is.

Coming along with me were a couple of Wizard teammates, DeShawn Stevenson and Brendan Haywood.

As I ran onto the court for my first game as a Maverick, Carlisle yelled, "Let's go get a championship."

High hopes, but I soon became a believer. We made it into the play-offs, and I wound up second on the team in scoring average in the post-season at 19.7 points per game, behind only Dirk Nowitzki.

Unfortunately, that was only for six games, because that's how long it took for San Antonio to bump us out in the first round.

But better times were ahead.

One of the joys of playing for the Mavs was the opportunity to talk to Mark Cuban all the time. We discussed things like the salary cap and how to invest my money. He was always talking about the business side of the game.

He was a different type of owner, young, spunky, cool. That's why everybody loved him.

In my first full season with the Mavs, my bad karma returned on the night of New Year's Day 2011 in Milwaukee, of all places, close to my hometown.

It was well over a third of the way through the regular season and things were going well. I had started all twenty-nine games in which I had played, averaging 15 points and shooting 45 percent from the floor.

But then, against the Bucks, it all ended, suddenly and unpredictably with a non-contact injury, the worst kind because, if you are hurt when another player is not involved, it means something inside your own body has broken down.

In my case, it was my right kneecap. I had planted my right leg, turned, and it collapsed. As I lay on the floor of the Bradley Center, it felt like my kneecap had popped out. I tried to slide it back into place with my hands as the trainer came running onto the floor.

Standing over me watching, all Dirk could say was, "Ohhhh," horrified at what he was seeing.

Still stretched out on the floor, I pounded the hardwood in frustration. Dirk, the team leader, was already out with a knee injury of his own. In his absence, I had been given the opportunity to step into his role, had responded well, and was coming off a 30-point performance against San Antonio in our last game.

Now this.

As I would soon learn, I had ruptured the patellar tendon in my right knee, a season-ending injury.

As I lay there on the floor, I thought about all my family and friends from nearby Racine in the crowd. I couldn't let them see me carried out on a stretcher or on the backs of teammates.

"Fuck it," I said and struggled to get on my feet.

"No, no, no, you can't get up," someone said.

I could and I did, tentatively planting my knee and walking off the court under my own power.

In the locker room, Mark Cuban was one of the first to get to me.

"Are you okay?" he asked.

"Don't worry about it," I told him. "Everything will be fine."

After the game, all my teammates came in, circled around me as I lay stretched out on a table, and told me to a man, "We are going to win it all for you."

After I had surgery to repair the knee, I came to every practice, every game, and off days in between to rehab. And I tried to heal quickly enough to come back before the season ended.

When we got into the playoffs, I desperately wanted to be part of everything. So I screamed on the sideline, yelled in the locker room, went to the shootarounds, and sat in on the film sessions. I tried to stay involved as if nothing had changed, but of course, there was one big change. I couldn't play.

I was there as we beat the Trail Blazers in six games, swept the Lakers, and eliminated the Thunder in five.

We faced my old team, the Heat, in the NBA Finals, which made it all the more bittersweet to sit on the bench.

With every passing game, my knee got stronger and stronger. Finally, my doctors decided that, if there was a Game 7, I would be able to suit up for limited minutes.

Instead, leading three games to two, we finished off Miami in Game 6 by a score of 105–95.

Still, I feel my ultimate goal of being on a championship team was realized. Obviously, I would have preferred to have been healthy and on the court, but my DNA was on that team. Because I have my fingerprints on the championship trophy, I can accept my role and roll with it. It's an opportunity most will never experience, so I regard that season as a true blessing.

And who knows, maybe I'll be fortunate enough to be on another title-winning team before my career is over.

That night, Mark Cuban took us all to a Miami club, Vivid Live, where he spent about $300,000. I don't know how you could spend $300,000 in one night at a club, but he did.

On the day of the championship parade through Dallas, as I stood on the podium with my teammates, I heard comments that will forever bond me with those guys. "You were our inspiration because you kept pushing, kept saying all the right things, motivating us," I was told. "We looked in your eyes and saw the determination."

I had one more memorable moment with the Mavs, but it happened after I had left through free agency to join the Clippers the following season. I had been looking forward to getting my championship ring, but the way it happened was unexpected, and so special.

Just before I came back to Dallas with the Clippers, my publicist, Kelly Swanson, tipped me off that I was going to get my ring before the game.

Sure enough, during the pregame introductions, the crowd was shown a video of my highlights over the season, from playing on the court to speaking from the podium at the end of the parade. Mark Cuban and Rick Carlisle took the mike and paid me some wonderful compliments. "You are a Mav for life," Carlisle told me. "You will always have a place in this organization."

Then, they handed me my ring. The ceremony meant a whole lot. It made me feel my effort and contributions didn't go unnoticed. That season was one for my bucket list. I always wanted to be part of something bigger than myself. That definitely was bigger.

I was real tight with a lot of the guys on that team like Dirk, Jason Kidd, Jason Terry, and Tyson Chandler along with DeShawn and Brendan, the guys who came with me from Washington. To this day, any time we see each other anywhere, our greeting is, "What's going on, champ." We are joined at the hip forever.

LOS ANGELES CLIPPERS

As a free agent following the 2010–2011 season, I was tempted to sign with the Nets. They were going to leave New Jersey for a new home in Brooklyn the following season, and I loved the idea of being part of such a historic move. I also loved the contract being dangled in front of me as well, four years for $34 million.

But what Andrea and I loved even more was the idea of coming back to L.A. and the great weather. Growing up in Wisconsin, I was always in search of blue skies.

Still, I was serious about the Nets, so serious that I was sitting with my agent, Raymond, in the office of their general manager, Billy King, talking about signing when Vinny Del Negro, the Clippers' coach, called me.

"We really want you," Vinny said. "We've got a deal for you to make about $8 million a year for three years."

Less money than New Jersey, but more sunshine.

"I can get on a plane, come out and talk," I said.

"Deal is ready," Vinny told me. "Just come out and sign it. It's done."

How could I say no? I didn't. Raymond and I left the meeting, flew to L.A., met with Vinny and Clipper general manager Neil Olshey in Marina Del Rey, and I signed the contract.

It was a wild time for the Clippers, unlike anything they had ever experienced in their nearly three decades of failure in L.A., always lost in the shadow of the Lakers. I got there a week before Chris Paul became a Clipper following Commissioner David Stern's decision to kill a deal that would have made Chris a Laker. Instead, he joined "the other team" in town and generated an exciting offense that soon earned the name Lob City. Rappers put that name in songs, fans and the media across the country referred to it all the time, and for the first time since they moved to L.A., the Clippers had their own identity, separate from the purple and gold. Along with Chris, we had players like Blake Griffin, DeAndre Jordan, and Chauncey Billups. Matt Barnes and Grant Hill came along in my second Clipper season, as did Lamar, who, through his marriage to Khloe, had the whole Kardashian thing going on. It was a circus, a real-life circus.

Chris and I really connected. We still text back and forth, communicating quite often. I see a lot of similarities between us as far as putting family first. On the court, he's a great floor general who gets everyone involved and keeps them engaged.

In 2012–2013, we won seventeen games in a row and the Pacific Division title for the first time in Clipper history to change the perception of the organization. But make no mistake about it, L.A. was still the Lakers' town. They've won sixteen championships, they've got all those banners in the rafters, they've got the tradition, and they've got the legacy of great players.

Still, nobody can say that the Clippers are not on the rise. They had a great season in 2014–2015. In Chris and Blake, they've got superstars in their prime; they've got a tremendous coach in Doc Rivers and now, in Steve Ballmer, they've got an owner with substantial wealth who is, I am confident, going to spare no expense in improving the product.

I'm happy that I was there to be part of the birth of this exciting new era in team history after the Clippers had suffered through so many decades of playing the Washington Generals to the Lakers' Harlem Globetrotters.

MILWAUKEE BUCKS

After two years with the Clippers, I was on the move again, traded to Phoenix in the summer of 2013 as part of a three-team deal. But if I had to leave L.A., I at least wanted to satisfy an unfulfilled wish to finally play at home.

To their credit, the Suns made that possible, trading me to the Bucks a little over a month later before I had even suited up for Phoenix.

Be careful what you wish for. I knew that playing in Milwaukee, where my dreams of being in the NBA had begun the night I saw Sidney Moncrief at the MECCA Arena, had already twice turned into nightmares. Prior to rupturing a patellar tendon in Milwaukee as a Mav, I had broken my right hand there, inadvertently smashing it against the backboard while trying to block a shot in 2007 as a member of the Wizards.

Don't get me wrong. It was a great experience playing at home on a regular basis during the season, but obligations come with that. Family and friends think, because you are home, you don't have to work, don't have to prepare. Being away, I got used to a certain structure and routine. Being home, I had to deal with every member of my family stopping by at one time or another. They were always right there. It became a little overwhelming at times for me and my wife and kids because the free time I did have, I ending up spending with everybody instead of primarily with my wife and children. They had to share me during the time I was in Milwaukee.

I normally never look in the crowd when I'm playing. When I come off the court, I may spot Halle Berry, Kim Kardashian, Jay-Z, or Beyonce. But when I'm in the game, I don't give a damn who's in the crowd because I'm dialed into what I'm doing. I block everything else out.

But when I was home, I always looked in the crowd. And I saw hundreds and hundreds of familiar faces, kids I went to grade school up to high school with, old teachers, people from the police department, and, of course, everybody in my family from my mom and my grandmother to my aunts, uncles, and their kids. Seeing close family members holding passes that allowed them to walk onto the court after the game gave me a great feeling because I knew I had made them feel special. That more than made up for any training time I lost by being home.

Larry Drew was my coach in Milwaukee. He was an honest man who took pride in his job, and that made the 2013–2014 season especially tough on him because the ownership was about to change and Drew was given orders to make sure a bad season didn't get any better before the draft. I think the Bucks were tanking from the beginning.

Drew told me, "Just go out there and score the ball. Have fun. The people of Wisconsin want to see you play, want to see you be successful."

That was great for me, but it ended up not being much fun because of all the losing.

What I most enjoyed about my time in Milwaukee was my role as a senior member of the squad. After all the seasons of being the young guy trying to learn from the veterans, now I was a leader passing on my knowledge to a new generation of guys. I showed teammates like John Henson and Ekpe Udoh my hometown, took them to the best places to eat, taught them how to be a professional, and talked to them about life on and off the court.

OKLAHOMA CITY THUNDER

With the Bucks' season going nowhere and a high ankle sprain limiting my effectiveness, I reached a buyout agreement with them with six weeks left in the season.

I had interest from several teams including the Heat. It would have been nice to have been reunited with Riles and Dwyane, but ultimately, I decided to go to the Thunder, a team with an excellent chance of winning the championship.

I came out a lot better than Drew. After the Bucks finished 15-67, he was fired, replaced by Jason Kidd. Drew is now an assistant coach for the Cavaliers.

The best part about joining the Thunder was playing with Kevin Durant. I had watched his development close up because he had played for Montrose Christian School in Rockville, Maryland, while I was in the neighborhood, playing for the Wizards.

Now, I was on the court with him as he enjoyed an MVP season. His performance night in and night out was no surprise to me. The day I joined the team, I wrote *K.D. MVP* on a piece of paper and handed it to him.

I knew what I was there for, to not only help him on the court, but also in terms of believing in himself. Even though he was universally ranked among the top two or three players in the game, K.D. still needed confirmation from those around him. It had to come from the older guys like Fish (Derek Fisher) and myself.

I got tears in my eyes when K.D. made his acceptance speech after winning the MVP award. He touched my heart talking about the sacrifices his mom had made to enable him to achieve success. He was telling my story as well. I could relate to coming from nothing and wanting everything, but being told you'd always be limited because of your circumstances, that you wouldn't ever have the opportunity to break the cycle of poverty.

But you build a bridge over the tears, hurdle the obstacles, see that all things are possible, and eventually reach your goals. That's what K.D. did with the help of not only his mom, but his brothers as well. He came from a deep place and that's why, when he told the world about it, so many people fell in love with him.

I felt bad when I heard at the end of the 2014–2015 season that Scott Brooks had been fired by the Thunder after seven seasons on the job. He was a really good coach, a players' coach, someone a player could always go to knowing that he had a totally open-door policy. He was a coach who not only talked, but listened.

When I was on the team, I almost felt like there were two coaches. Although Fish went on to become a head coach with the Knicks, I felt like he was already a coach when I played with him. It's not that he undercut Brooks's authority in any way. Far from it. But Fish was so smart about the game, so poised, so positive, so unflappable in his demeanor regardless of the situation, so articulate and wise in his remarks to both teammates and the media, and so respected because he was a highly decorated veteran that he commanded everyone's attention. I had a great relationship with him and still do, texting him throughout his first season as a coach, telling him to keep his head up and never stop pushing. It had to be tough, struggling in the biggest media market in the country, but I know of no one who could have done a better job of handling the pressure.

DETROIT PISTONS

When I signed a two-year, $10 million contract with the Pistons before the 2014–2015 season, I felt like I had come full circle. I was back where I had started, playing under Stan Van Gundy, Riles's disciple.

Van Gundy reminds me of Max in terms of passion about his craft and philosophy about the game. It can be a challenge playing for Van Gundy because he is still the same loud, animated coach, a screamer when necessary, but always an inspirational teacher.

There is young talent on that team, guys who are on the cusp of becoming really special players. But Van Gundy knows that, for them to be successful, they've got to be confident enough to believe in themselves and the team.

It's tough because it's been a while since the Pistons' franchise has had a winning culture. The right things haven't been instilled in the players in the past, so they have been forced to learn on the fly. But they are coming along.

The fact that we were able to pull ourselves out of a 5-23 start and even be in the discussion about a playoff spot says a lot about the guys on the team.

I embraced my role as a senior member of the club while I was there. Yes, I've had to sacrifice playing time so that the younger guys could get more experience, but I'm happy that I'm still seen as a valuable asset at the age of thirty-five.

SACRAMENTO KINGS

Free agency can be a tricky thing. When I became a free agent in the summer of 2015, I wanted to sign with the team that gave me my best chance of getting another championship ring. But I didn't want to be one of four or five guys auditioning for one remaining roster spot on the Spurs or the Cavs.

So when Vlad Divac, now a Kings vice president, and Peja Stojakovic, who is helping Vlad and was a teammate of mine on the Mavs, approached me about signing with Sacramento, I listened.

Intrigued after talking to Kings owner Vivek Ranadive and coach George Karl about plans to restore a winning culture in Sacramento and give me a role as both player and mentor to the young guys, I agreed to a two-year deal.

It was a long, difficult climb from the hard floor of a cell in solitary confinement in Ethan Allen to the hardwood of the NBA. I am proud to have made that climb, to have lasted thirteen seasons with still more to come, to have earned enough money to make life easier and more fulfilling for my family, and to have hopefully made conditions better in Racine for all who come after me.

This is the life I dreamed of as a kid, but the reality has been far more wonderful than I could have ever imagined.

Epilogue

The best part of my career has been the happiness, security, and good health it has brought those closest to me: my wonderful wife, Andrea, and our three precious daughters, Mia Caron, Ava Caron, and Gia Caron; my daughter, Camary, and son, Caron Jr., from previous relationships; and, of course, my wonderful mom, grandmother, and brother.

When I was a little kid watching NBA games with my grandmother on her little TV, I told her that I was going to be running up and down the court like MJ when I got older and I would buy her a big TV to watch me.

That came true, of course. I love giving gifts and making life comfortable for my mom and grandmother. Without all the years of grueling hours and hard labor they endured, my life would have turned out vastly different, and not in a good way. That is, if I had not lost my life on the streets.

But the biggest gift I ever gave my grandmother was the gift of life.

Several years ago, I began to notice that the color in her face was not good.

When I mentioned it to her, my grandmother would just joke, saying, "No, I'm black and beautiful."

But this was no joke. There was a yellowish tinge to her complexion. Having spent time with Alonzo Mourning during my seasons in Miami, I knew this could be a sign of kidney problems.

Using FaceTime, I got Alonzo and a doctor in DC to look at my grandmother. They felt she needed to undergo a medical exam immediately.

Despite her insistence that she was fine, I flew her to Georgetown University in DC to see a kidney specialist, who determined that she needed a transplant.

In another few months, it might be too late, she was told.

My grandmother had the transplant in 2011 and now has a complexion that is again black and beautiful.

I have lost too many good people in my life. I am thankful that she was saved.

It is because of someone like you that we have something to strive for.
—From an incarcerated felon

Seeing the things you have accomplished after all you have been through shows me that hope never dies.
—From a young kid

You have helped me understand a lot of things without even knowing me.
—From a fan named Michael

The messages above are just a sample of the many I've received over the years from people who have been affected by my story.

They and so many others have inspired me to write this book. It is a chance to use the unique platform I have been given through my fame as a basketball player to reach the many other Caron Butlers out there, kids who are born into tough circumstances and can't see past their street corner. When you are not exposed to anything beyond the confines of your environment, you feel you can't become more than the people around you—the drug dealers, pimps, and hustlers. That's all that you see, that's all that you can be.

The conditions in neighborhoods like the one I grew up in breed cynicism and pessimism. I was part of that mind-set as a kid. We all felt that dudes like us who sold drugs, lived on welfare, and were involved with gangs were never going to live a better life.

I want to expand the horizon of kids who grew up like I did. I hope my story can do that by enabling them to learn from it and write their own success stories.

I know some will say it's easy for me to talk about success because I've been blessed with the talent to be an NBA player. A lot of people judge your glory without knowing your story.

But when they hear my story, kids will realize it can happen to them as well. Somebody else who went through what they are going through, somebody surrounded by crime and poverty, trapped on streets that led nowhere, made it out of the ghetto. It can be done.

Once I got a different view of life and positive feedback, once I was embraced by those who showed me a better path than the one I was on, a world of opportunity opened up for me.

I've made millions of dollars doing something that I love. This book can be another opportunity for me to give back. I mean that from the bottom of my heart.

Much of the stuff I do now is to make up for what I did in the past. I make time to spend with kids, helping to improve their lives because I used to spend a lot of time in the streets selling other kids poison. Now, I give away bikes, stage a coat-giveaway day, and do whatever else I can for the less fortunate.

Still, I always feel like I could do a little more, because I always did a little more when I was in the streets. I would go the extra mile to find somebody to buy my drugs. So why shouldn't I go the extra mile now to sell hope?

I've sold it to those closest to me. Because of the money I have made in the NBA, I've been able to provide for both my immediate and extended family. But of even more importance, I will have been able to change the thought process and culture of my family for generations to come. Those who are here now will bear witness to all who follow. They are believers because they've seen it firsthand. They've watched me go from drug dealing, gangbanging, and solitary confinement to being a role model in my community.

It's a role I take very seriously. I feel I can affect not just young basketball players, but anybody in search of the road to redemption.

There's an old saying that I first heard from my grandmother. She would often tell me, "You can give a man a fish and feed him for a day. Or, you can teach a man to fish and feed him for a lifetime."

I have embraced that philosophy in dealing with family and friends in my community.

Yes, I have the money that can benefit those I care about. But I don't believe simply giving it away is the answer.

Andrea and I came out to our car one night in Racine and found that somebody had put a rubber band around all of their bills—rent, credit cards, food—and left them on our windshield. You're an NBA player, they were, in effect, telling me. Paying my bills would be easy for you.

That's true, but it's not a solution because, next month, that person would have another stack of bills.

"You probably won't earn the type of living that I do," I tell family and friends, "but you can earn *a* living. Find your niche. Like me, find something that you are good at and that you are passionate about so that every day, when you wake up, you can't wait to go to work because you don't consider it work.

"If you need to go to school to pursue your chosen career in order to get a certificate or to qualify for a license, do it. Then come to me because I may be able to hook you up with the right person to make this happen for you."

For many years in my neighborhood, people felt there were only two alternatives for making money, assembly-line work or selling crack. But it's changing now.

Even if it turns out that I can't help, at least those who followed my advice will have gotten an education, which will surely open up other career paths.

My goal is to help create as many success stories as I can on the south side of Racine, to enable others to experience the happy ending enjoyed by Junebug.

The former drug kingpin of Racine is now forty-four. Seventeen of those years were spent in prison.

When Junebug got out after his final incarceration, I was playing in Washington. He and his wife, my Aunt Kathy, moved there from Racine to get out of the line of fire from the drug wars.

I got Junebug a job at a company that remodeled houses, visited their offices, handed out game tickets, did whatever I could to make him look good to his bosses.

Today, with a little seed money from me, Junebug has his own construction company in Racine. Like he always says, he doesn't make as much money as he did heading a drug-dealing operation, but he gets to come home at night.

I once sent Detective Rick Geller a text that read, "Your impact on my life is everlasting."

He texted me back, "And you pass it on."

That's what I'm devoted to doing, passing it on for the rest of my life.

Some of the ways Caron Butler is passing it on:

While a member of the Wizards, Butler was a regular visitor at the Oak Hill Youth Detention Center in Laurel, Maryland, spending time with inmates.

He also visited injured soldiers at the Walter Reed Medical Center in Washington, DC.

He helped organize "Urban Dialogue: Stop the Violence," a community outreach event in Racine.

Butler sponsored the Racine "Cops 'N Kids" Legacy Project, a program that enables police officers to distribute books to youngsters, and created a reading center where kids can read or borrow books, use computers, and receive one-on-one tutoring.

He teamed up with the Salvation Army and Walmart to sponsor the "Bike Brigade," a program that distributes new bikes and helmets to youngsters in Racine and Washington, DC. So far, over 2,500 bikes have been given out.

He created "Caron's Coats for Kids," supplying coats, hats, and gloves to youngsters in both Racine and DC.

He established Butler Elite Basketball, an AAU organization in Racine that provides life-skill training, supportive coaching, and academic tutoring.

In 2007, Butler joined Tobacco Free Families and helped to launch a quit smoking campaign. He teamed with DC United player Facundo Erpen as well as the DC City Council to announce a $10 million tobacco prevention and cessation campaign.

Butler and his wife, Andrea, were given the 2007 Conversation Changers Award by the DC Campaign to prevent teenage pregnancy.

Butler won the NBA's Community Assist Award for June 2007 in recognition of his work in the community and for his ongoing philanthropic contributions.

In 2008, he traveled to Johannesburg, South Africa, as a part of the NBA's Basketball without Borders delegation. Along with several other players, he visited schools, conducted basketball clinics, and talked with local youngsters about the importance of following their dreams and making good decisions.

In 2009, Butler organized "Caron's 3D Summer Explosion," a program that included events almost every weekend for Racine kids, including an organized day of service, a free basketball clinic, a charity game, and a back-to-school supply drive.

In 2012, he donated $200,000 to the Racine United Way, George Bray Center, Juneteenth Foundation, and YMCA organizations.

For passing it on, his honors include a Caron Butler Day in Racine, a Caron Butler Day in Connecticut, being named Role Model of the Year by the Connecticut Middlesex County Chamber of Commerce, and being given the Good Brother Award by the National Congress of Black Women.

Acknowledgments

People have been telling me for years that my journey from the streets to the NBA would make a great book and provide hope for so many others who feel trapped in an environment similar to the one I grew up in.

Once I actually sat down to do this book, it caused me to reflect on my life and all those who have helped me on this journey. Believe me, I didn't do it alone. So many others are deserving of my deep gratitude.

It begins, as do all things, with God. His presence makes everything possible.

I have to start off by thanking my mom, an amazing person who raised me as a single mom, exposed me to everything she could, and inspired me to be all I could be. Without her sacrifice, none of this would be possible.

I want to thank my grandma for filling in the void as a father and helping raise me.

I want to thank my wife, the love of my life, for always being there for me through highs and lows, injuries, everything. Always being my better half. When she gave birth to our firstborn, Mia, it gave me new life! Then along came our other two daughters, Ava and Gia, to bring us even more joy.

To my aunts and uncles, Amy, Tina, Kathy, Clarice, Richard, and Carlos: Thank you all for having such a positive impact on my life and helping mold me into the man I am today.

To my agent, Raymond Brothers, the same agent I have had since Day 1: My family thanks you for being so reliable.

Others deserving of my sincere love and gratitude are:

My other children from previous relationships, Camary and Caron Jr., my little brother, Melvin Jr., my many aunts and uncles, and Andrea's wonderful family, the Pinks.

My cousin Kailo Butler, who was killed in a car accident. Gone but never forgotten, her name tattooed on my left arm, her memory tattooed in my heart.

Ricardo Dawkins and my other bloodline cousins.

Jamie Harris, who fronted me the money to go to prep school.

Junebug, Black Rob, Li'l Greg, Andre Love, Andre King, and all the other guys I hung with at the Bryant Center, the Bray Center, and on the streets of Racine.

Kobe Bryant.

Kevin Durant.

Dwyane Wade.

NBA commissioner Adam Silver, the owners and front-office personnel I've played for, and all the teammates I played with in the league.

My many coaches through the years: Walley Rhome, Bart Trussel, Rudy Collum, Doug Whitely, Jim Betker, Jameel Ghuari, Max Good at Maine Central Institute, Jim Calhoun at UConn, and all my NBA coaches from Pat Riley to Stan Van Gundy. Eddie Jordan gets special mention for naming me Tuff Juice.

My teammates and the assistant coaches at UConn, and all the wonderful friends Andrea and I had on campus.

Rosalyn Johnson, a schoolteacher who encouraged me to be great, Detective Rick Geller, who gave me a second chance, and Racine chief of police Art Howell, who has devoted his career to keeping the streets of Racine safe.

My publicist, Kelly Swanson.

Nike representative Nico Harris, who has always been there for me.

United Way and Youth for Christ for all they do.

Pak's Jewelers for keeping me in style.

I will never again look at a book on a shelf without understanding all the people and all the effort it took to get it there. So many people have contributed to the production of *Tuff Juice* and I'd like to thank a few:

Steve Springer, who helped me write it.

Kobe again, for writing the foreword.

My literary agent, Dana Newman, who sold the book.

Tabrez Yousuf of I AM Sports & Entertainment, Carmen Wilson, and Britney Thompson, who did all the heavy lifting in terms of collecting pictures, setting up interviews, negotiating expenses, handling travel arrangements, and doing whatever else was necessary to make this project a success.

Keith Wallman and the crew at Lyons Press, the people who are producing this book.

And finally, to Racinehistory.com and the Wisconsin Historical Society, the sources for much of my information about the history of the area.

Seeing is believing, hard work pays off, and God is good all the time.

Be blessed,
Caron Butler

Index

About the Coauthors

Caron Butler is a veteran NBA All-Star and a dedicated member of the community. He is extremely active with organizations that specialize in youth outreach, especially in his hometown of Racine, Wisconsin. In addition to his extensive philanthropy, Butler is also a burgeoning businessman with plans to own an NBA team. He lives in Beverly Hills, California.

Steve Springer is the author and coauthor of twelve books including a *New York Times* bestseller, *American Son: My Story*—Oscar De La Hoya's autobiography—and two *Los Angeles Times* bestsellers. He lives in Woodland Hills, California.